A Leader's Guide to Activities for Girls Ages 8 to 11

Amy Peterson

Walnut Springs Press, LLC
110 South 800 West
Brigham City, Utah 84302
http://walnutspringspress.blogspot.com

ISBN: 978-1-935217-90-9

Contents

Scripture Skit or Play

What You Will Need

- Various costumes (Nativity costumes would work great)
- Various props

What to Do

Bring a bag of miscellaneous props and costumes. Have the girls use the props to come up with their own scripture story. They can even do fun variations, such as Danielle (instead of Daniel) in the lion's den meets the good Samaritan.

Scriptionary

What You Will Need

- Scriptionary cards, prepared ahead of time

What to Do

This game is like Pictionary, only it is played with scripture references. On each of several 3 x 5-inch cards, write the scripture reference for a different scripture story. For each card, have some girls look up the scripture and draw clues while other girls guess the story.

Variation

Write scripture story or word on card, but do not give the scripture reference. Example: Daniel and the lion's den, the Liahona, the Book of Mormon.

To Save You Time

Genesis 41:43 (Ruler)
Psalms 27:1 (Light)
Psalms 119:105 (Lamp)
Genesis 28:12 (Ladder)
Proverbs 24:26 (Kiss or lips)
Proverbs 23:2 (Knife)
Genesis 49:24 (Rock)
Genesis 1:11 (Grass)
Alma 37:38 (The Liahona)
Proverbs 1:14 (Purse)
1 Samuel 17:23 (David and Goliath)

Exodus 8:2 (Frogs)
Genesis 3:3 (Tree)
Isaiah 40:6 (Flower)
Exodus 7:21 (Fish)
Exodus 32:2 (Earrings)
Matthew 14:20 (Basket)
Proverbs 31:18 (Candle)
Genesis 7:7 (Noah and the ark)
Genesis 3:19 (Bread)
Exodus 34:28 (Ten Commandments)
Daniel 6:16 (Daniel and the lion's den)

Scripture Cookies

What You Will Need

- Ingredients for cookies
- Large bowl
- Large spoon
- Cookie sheet
- Spatula
- Zip-top plastic bags
- Large paper bag or cardboard box

What to Do

You will need to look up the scripture references ahead of time. You may also want to premeasure each dry ingredient and place it in a zip-top plastic bag. When girls arrive, have them sit around the table where you have placed the bowl and spoon. Hide the ingredients in a paper bag or in a cardboard box under the table. Start out by giving a scripture reference that relates to the first ingredient in the cookies. Girls must look up the scripture to find the hint. When they correctly guess the ingredient, put it in the bowl, then move on to the next scripture reference and ingredient. When all ingredients are in the bowl, mix up the cookies.

While cookies are baking, share your favorite scripture stories with the girls. Explain why Heavenly Father and Jesus Christ want us to read the scriptures.

Scripture Cookie Recipe

1 cup Psalms 55:21 (butter)
½ cup Jeremiah 6:20 (white sugar)
1 cup Jeremiah 6:20 (brown sugar)
two Isaiah 10:14 (eggs)
2 teaspoons 2 Chronicles 9:9 (vanilla)
1¼ cups Numbers 28:5 (flour)
½ teaspoon Amos 4:5 (baking soda)
1 teaspoon 3 Nephi 12:13 (salt)
3 cups Doctrine and Covenants 89:17 (oatmeal)
1 cup 1 Samuel 30:12 (raisins, or you can use chocolate chips)

Mix together Psalms, Jeremiah, Isaiah, and Chronicles. Then add Numbers, 3 Nephi, and Amos, then mix in D&C and Samuel. Roll into 1-inch balls and put on a greased cookie sheet. Bake about 12 minutes at 325°F. Let cool, eat, enjoy!

Scripture Time

What You Will Need

- Small (6 x 9-inch) manila envelopes
- Typed list of scriptures to be memorized

What to Do

Have each girl make a pocket using a manila envelope (they also come in white). Cut a few inches off the top of the envelope to create a pocket. Have the girls decorate the front of the pocket. Then punch a hole at the top of each corner of the pocket. Take a piece of ribbon and tie each end to one of the holes, creating a handle. Type a list of scriptures the girls can memorize. Have the girls cut them into strips and put them in their scripture pockets. Have each girl hang the pocket on her bedroom doorknob or somewhere else where she'll see it. Have the girls memorize as many as they can in a month (or six weeks), or have a contest to see who can learn the most scriptures.

Variations

- Make a chart where each girl can check off each scripture as she memorizes it.

Make a Scripture Bag

What You Will Need

- Plain canvas bag (available at Oriental Trading Company or most craft stores) for each girl
- Red scripture-marking pencil for each girl
- Various items to decorate bags (for example, fabric markers, fabric paint, buttons, foam shapes)

What to Do

Have each girl decorate her bag. Have a lesson about reading the scriptures every day, the importance of the scriptures, and bringing one's scriptures to church every week. Give each girl a red pencil, and show the girls how to use their scriptures.

Scripture Trivia

This is a great way to test your Activity Days girls' scripture knowledge.

What You Will Need

- Scripture story trivia questions

What to Do

Ask the girls various scripture trivia questions. Divide girls into teams or have everyone play against each other.

To Save You Time

Who was the first man on earth? Adam
Who built an ark? Noah
Why did the Lord ask Noah to build an ark? To protect his family from the flood that would kill all the wicked people.
Who was put into a basket in the river as a baby, to protect him? Moses
Who was Goliath? A Philistine soldier, a giant of a man.
How tall was Goliath? Over 9 feet
What did Daniel refuse to eat? The king's meat and wine
What did Daniel ask to eat? Grain and water
Why did Moses make a brass serpent? To save those who had been bitten by the fiery serpents that were sent to punish the wicked.
Where did Jesus grow up? Nazareth

Variation

Tell various scripture stories. Then ask girls trivia questions about the stories. Give girls the assignment the week before to read certain scripture stories and be prepared to answer trivia questions at the next activity. If you want, copy the back of the Gospel Art pictures (found in your meetinghouse library or at LDS Distribution Centers) for your scripture stories, and send them home with each girl to read before the activity.

Book of Mormon Scripture Hunt

What You Will Need

- List of scriptures or scripture cards

What to Do

Take the girls to a local park or go for a walk around the neighborhood. Give each girl a scripture to look up. Have each girl read her particular scripture before you leave, to figure out what item she needs to find on the hunt. (That way the girls don't need to bring their scriptures to the park.)

To Save You Time

Clues for Book of Mormon Scripture Hunt

Jacob 5:16 (tree)
Psalms 72:6 (grass)
Flower: Exodus 25:34 (flower)
Alma 7:19 (path)
2 Nephi 14:1 (bread to feed ducks)
1 Nephi 8:32 (fountain [drinking fountain])
2 Nephi 4:30 (rock)
Ether 2:2 (fish)
2 Nephi 15:6 (thorns/weeds)
1 Nephi 20:19 (sand)
1 Nephi 8:19 (rod of iron [monkey bars])
1 Nephi 8:26 (building in the air [treehouse])

Variation

Take the girls to the Church meetinghouse or someone's house. Give each girl a scripture to look up and split girls into teams. Have each girl read the scripture to figure out what item she needs to find on the hunt. Hide some items ahead of time that you may not find at your meetinghouse or someone's home.

Clues for Scripture Hunt

Exodus 17:2 (water to drink)
Mark 8:14 (bread)
Ezekiel 27:6 (bench)
Mark 9:49 (salt)
2 Nephi 27:6 (book)
1 Nephi 8:10 (fruit)

Proverbs 25:11 (apples)
Acts 9:25 (basket)
Ezekiel 40:39 (table)
Ezekiel 41:2 (door)

Scripture Version I-spy Bottle

What You Will Need

- Plastic bottle (a 20-ounce drink bottle works great)
- Hot glue gun
- Filler for the bottle (birdseed, rice, or bean-bag pellets)
- Scripture references (see below) typed on paper and laminated
- Ribbon
- Items listed below (find them at craft, hardware, discount, dollar, or party-supply stores)
    - Ring or piece of fabric (Genesis 41:42)
    - Dog or pig (Matthew 7:6)
    - Bird or fake leaf (Genesis 8:11)
    - Nail (3 Nephi 11:14)
    - Pearl (Matthew 13:46)
    - Bear, cow, or lion; drinking straw cut into thirds (Isaiah 11:7)
    - Sun (D&C 76:70)
    - Christmas tree light or candle (Psalms 27:1)
    - Small plastic or wooden star (D&C 76:81)
    - Ruby plastic jewel, or red bead or button (Proverbs 31:10)
    - Toy wheel or horse (Isaiah 5:28)
    - Heart (Matthew 5:8)
    - Bee (Ether 2:3)
    - Large (about 3/8”) googly eye (D&C 88:67)
    - Clear or white rock (Ether 3:1)

What to Do

Fill plastic bottle with the trinkets, then pour in filler until it is within an inch of the top of the bottle. Put hot glue on the threads of the bottleneck, then put lid on. Tie laminated cheat sheet around top of bottle.

Variation

Trinket ideas for Gospel Standards (look in *Faith in God* book for exact wording of standards)

- Follow Heavenly Father's plan: miniature shoe or foot
- Remember baptismal covenant and listen to the Holy Ghost: white fabric
- Choose the right, and repent after making a mistake: small eraser
- Be honest with Heavenly Father, others, and self: miniature bee or letter B ("I will 'b' [or 'bee'] honest.")
- Do not take the Lord's name in vain, swear, or use crude words: smiley face
- Keep the Sabbath day holy and stay close to Heavenly Father and Jesus: a penny (because we pay tithing on Sunday).
- Honor parents and help strengthen family: puzzle piece (keep family together)
- Keep mind and body pure and sacred, and do not partake of harmful things: small fruit
- Dress modestly to show respect for Heavenly Father and self: plain button
- Read and watch things that are pleasing to Heavenly Father: googly eye
- Only listen to music that is pleasing to Heavenly Father: small bell or musical note
- Have good friends and treat others kindly: plastic heart
- Live now to be worthy to go to the temple, serve a mission, and do our part to have an eternal family: birthday candle or Christmas tree light. (You will walk in the light to prepare for the temple and your eternal family.)

Article-of-Faith Flip-Chart or Scripture Cards

What You Will Need

- Cardstock for printing scriptures or Articles of Faith
- Printer
- Book rings
- Colored pencils or markers to decorate (optional)

What to Do

Type the thirteen Articles of Faith on two 8.5 x 11-inch pieces of paper, with each article in its own square. Put the first through the eighth articles on one page (or fewer, depending on how big you want them), and the rest on the second page. You will have extra squares on the second page, so use one as a cover and one as a back page. (Instead of typing each Article of Faith, you can copy and paste each one from the scripture section of lds.org.) Have the girls cut out squares and decorate them, then attach all of them together using a book ring. (Book rings can be found in various sizes at office supply stores and at many discount or grocery stores.) You can also use seminary Scripture Mastery scriptures—it is never too early to memorize them! Laminate the Articles of Faith squares if possible.

Variation

Make a card for each girl. The card will say, "Article of Faith Card" and the girl's name. Have the numbers 1 through 13 along the outside of the card. You can make these on a computer and print on cardstock, or take large or small index cards and write up your own. When a girl passes off one of the Articles of Faith, mark off that number on her card. To mark them off, use a decorative hole punch, a plain hole punch, a marker, or small stickers.

Articles of Faith Trivia

What You Will Need

- Trivia cards about the Articles of Faith

What to Do

Use a Trivial Pursuit game board. Type your questions on a piece of paper and cut into squares, or glue on index cards. Now have the girls play Trivial Pursuit, Articles of Faith version, using the cards you made. (Optional: Put questions on colored index cards or colored paper. Assign each category a different color [for example, Articles of Faith 1–4, 5–8, etc.].) Or combine with other gospel doctrines and make each one a different color/category (for example, prophets, scripture stories, Articles of Faith, etc.).

Variations

- Read the questions out loud and see who can answer them first.
- Pass out worksheets with the trivia questions and have each girl answer the questions herself. Works great as a time filler at an activity, or to keep girls entertained as you wait for all of them to arrive.

To Save You Time

Joseph Smith wrote 13 statements called the __________ of Faith.

The second word in twelve of the Articles of Faith is ____________.

In the eleventh Article of Faith, the second word is different from the other Articles of Faith. What is the word? ____________

"We claim the privilege of worshipping Almighty God according to the ______ of our own conscience."

How many times is the word "prophecy" used in the Articles of Faith?

"We believe in . . . doing _______ to all men."

The first part of the thirteenth Article of Faith states, "We believe in being ________."

"We believe in the literal gathering of ___________."

"We believe . . . that Zion (the New ___________) will be built upon the American continent."

Which Article of Faith contains the word *kingdom?*

"We believe all that God __________ reveal."

"We believe in the same _____ that existed in the Primitive Church."

"We believe that a man must be called of God, by ____________."

Whose sins will we be punished for?

"We believe in the gift of tongues, prophecy,__________ visions . . ."

"We believe the Bible to be the word of God as far as it is ______________ correctly."

"We believe . . . that Christ will reign personally upon the _______."

Which standard works are the Articles of Faith found in?

"We believe all that God has revealed, all that He does now reveal, and we believe that He will yet reveal many _______ and important things pertaining to the kingdom of God."

Game: First Letters of the Articles of Faith

What You Will Need

- Papers, flashcards, or posters that display the first letter of each word of an Article of Faith

What to Do

Make a "worksheet" for each girl. Have the girls use the clues (first letter of each word of an Article of Faith) to write down the Articles of Faith. (Do six at one activity and the remaining six at another activity.)

To Save You Time

Article of Faith 1: W B I G T E F A I H S J C A I T H G

Article of Faith 2: W B T M W B P F T O S A N F A T

Article of Faith 3: W B T T T A O C A M M B S B O T T L A O O T G

Article of Faith 4: W B T T F P A O O T G A F F I T L J C S R T B B I F T R O S F L O O H F T G O T H G

Article of Faith 5: W B T A M M B C O G B P A B T L O O H B T W A I A T P T G A A I T O T

Article of Faith 6: W B I T S O T E I T P C N A P P T E A S F

Article of Faith 7: W B I T G O T P R V H I O T A S F

Article of Faith 8: W B T B T B T W O G A F A I I T C W A B T B O M T B T W O G

Article of Faith 9: W B A T G H R A T H D N R A W B T H W Y R M G A I T P T T K O G

Article of Faith 10: W B I T L G O I A I T R O T T T T Z T N J W B B U T A C T C W R P U T E A T T E W B R A R I P G

Article of Faith 11: W C T P O W A G A T T D O O O C A A A M T S P L T W H W O W T M

Article of Faith 12: W B I B S T K P R A M I O H A S T L

Article of Faith 13: W B I B H T C B V A I D G T A M I W M S T W F T A O P W B A T W H A T W H E M T A H T B A T E A T I T I A V L O O G R O P W S A T T

Articles of Faith Magnets

What You Will Need

- Rolls of magnetic strips or printable magnetic paper (available at office supply stores or craft stores such as Michaels)
- Pens or thin felt-tip permanent markers (test to make sure they write on magnets)
- For each girl, a container for storing magnets, such as a small jar or box (you may want to ask girls to bring their own containers)
- Materials for decorating containers

What to Do

Have the girls make magnets that will help them memorize the Articles of Faith. To start, each girl picks the Article of Faith with which she needs the most help. Put one or two words of the Article of Faith on each magnet. After, have girls decorate the containers for their magnets. Tell girls they can put the entire Article of Faith on a fridge or magnet board at home, then gradually take off word strips as they are memorized. Soon girls will be able to recite the Articles of Faith without using the magnetic strips. Can make additional Article of Faith magnets at different activities.

Articles of Faith Blocks

What You Will Need

- Blocks (the blocks from the game Jenga would work great)
- Strips of paper with Articles of Faith printed on them

What to Do

In advance, type some of the thirteen Articles of Faith onto strips of paper that are smaller in width than the blocks you have. Cut the Articles of Faith into pieces that will fit on the blocks. Put the blocks on the table and have the girls try to put together as many of the Articles of Faith as they can.

Articles of Faith Matchup

What You Will Need

- Game pieces—cards with each Article of Faith number (for example, 13), and separate cards with Article of Faith keywords or clues (see "To Save You Time").

What to Do

Hide the game pieces around the room. Have the girls try to find them and match them up, or play a memory game with the clues (like Concentration). Have girls recite the entire Article of Faith as a group when they make a match.

To Save You Time

Article of Faith 1: Godhead
Article of Faith 2: Punished
Article of Faith 3: Atonement
Article of Faith 4: First principles
Article of Faith 5: Called of God
Article of Faith 6: Organization
Article of Faith 7: Gift of tongues
Article of Faith 8: Translated
Article of Faith 9: Revealed
Article of Faith 10: Ten Tribes
Article of Faith 11: We claim
Article of Faith 12: Kings
Article of Faith 13: Virtuous

Gospel Hot Potato

What You Will Need

- Bean bag or small ball

What to Do

Have the girls sit in a circle. Have them toss the ball or bean bag to each other. When a girl catches the ball or bean bag, she must name a prophet (either past or present). You can also use this same concept using temples, scripture stories, etc.

Variations

- Play the same game but with music. When the music stops, whoever is holding the ball or bean bag names a prophet.
- Have each girl name something unique about herself, a talent she has, or something nice about the person on her left or right.

Where Were the Prophets Baptized?

What You Will Need

- Locations of various prophets' baptisms
- Fun facts about the prophets' baptisms

What to Do

Teach the girls about each prophet's baptism, and then have a matching game. Match each prophet to where he was baptized.

To Save You Time

Jesus: River Jordan

Joseph Smith: Susquehanna River

Brigham Young: his own millpond near Mendon, New York

John Taylor: Black Creek in Ontario, Canada

Wilford Woodruff: an icy stream near Richland, New York

Lorenzo Snow: Chagrin River in Kirtland, Ohio

George Albert Smith: City Creek in Salt Lake City, Utah

Heber J. Grant: a wagon box in Salt Lake City, Utah

Spencer W. Kimball: a hog-scalding tub that was also used as the family's bathtub

Howard W. Hunter: (at age 12, after getting permission from his father) an indoor swimming pool in Idaho

Concentration to Learn about the Prophets

What You Will Need

- Pictures of modern and ancient prophets
- Information about prophets, or quotes from prophets

What to Do

Make your own Concentration game that teaches about the prophets. To make it easy, use pictures from the Gospel Art Kit. Cover side with writing with a piece of colored paper. Using separate pieces of colored paper, write facts about prophets of whom you have pictures. Number the back of each paper and tape them in random order on a chalkboard or wall. Now have girls pick two numbers, trying to make a match between a prophet and his quote or information. When girls make a match, leave both papers right side out. Continue doing this until all the pictures are matched.

Variations

- Make the game using temples (match picture of temple with name of temple). Or use the Articles of Faith (match Article of Faith with its number, or match first half with second half).
- Have the girls write each book in the Book of Mormon on a separate index card. Then have them practice putting them in the correct order.

To Save You Time

Adam: first prophet

Noah: built an ark

Moses: freed the Israelites

Samuel the Lamanite: preached the word of God on a wall

Daniel: survived in the lion's den
Enoch: a prophet whose city was taken up into heaven
Samuel: a prophet chosen as a boy
Moroni: abridged the golden plates
Abinadi: was burned at the stake for his testimony
Heleman: commanded the 2000 stripling warriors
Joseph Smith Jr.: restored the gospel on the earth
Brigham Young: guided Saints to Salt Lake Valley
Lorenzo Snow: known for his strong testimony of tithing
Joseph F. Smith: taught Church members to have family home evening
Heber J. Grant: helped the Saints through World War I and II
George Albert Smith: enjoyed Scouting and camping
David O. McKay: said, "Every member a missionary."
Joseph Fielding Smith: called to the Quorum of the Twelve by his father, Joseph F. Smith
Ezra Taft Benson: encouraged Church members to read the Book of Mormon
Gordon B. Hinckley: dedicated 92 temples
Thomas S. Monson: raised pigeons as a boy

Follow the Prophet

What You Will Need

- Recent general conference talk by the President of the Church (purchase the DVD of general conference, or download a talk at lds.org)

What to Do

Watch a general conference talk by the prophet. Have each girl answer questions on a sheet of paper shaped like a footprint. Then have the girls lay down the footprints and follow them to a painting of the Savior. Talk about how people sometimes leave a trail of food when someone needs to follow them. Serve treats or other candies that could be used to leave a trail.

To Save You Time
http://lds.org/conference/languages/0,6353,310-1,00.html

Personal History

What You Will Need
- Notebook for each girl to use as a journal

What to Do
Challenge girls to keep a personal journal for a month. Talk about how the Lord has commanded us to keep records and keep a personal history.

Variation
Have each girl write her personal history, or make a collage of special things about her and her history.

Create a Personal or Family Coat of Arms

What You Will Need
- A book or website in which to look up the coat of arms for each girl (by her last name)
- Paper or cardstock
- Markers, crayons, colored pencils, or paint
- Scissors
- Glue
- Fake jewels, beads etc.

What to Do
Teach the girls about heraldry. (Heraldry is the practice of devising, blazoning, and granting armorial insignia and of tracing and recording genealogies.) Help each girl design and create a personal or family coat of arms.

To Save You Time
http://www.allfamilycrests.com/
http://www.ancestorhunt.com/family-coat-of-arms.htm

Ancestor Dolls

What You Will Need

- Clothespins or popsicle sticks
- Yarn
- Fabric or paper scraps
- Markers
- Glue
- Poster boards

What to Do

Using the clothespins or popsicle sticks, have each girl make a doll to represent four generations. Using a poster board, make a pedigree chart, and glue or tape each ancestor doll in the appropriate place.

Decorate Frames for Proclamation of the Family

What You Will Need

- Frames (craft foam, papier maché, or wood)
- Items to decorate frames (markers, glue, craft jewels, buttons foam shapes, stickers, etc.)
- Glue or glue dots
- Copy of "The Family: A Proclamation to the World" for each girl (free online or at LDS Distribution Center)

What to Do

Let each girl decorate her own frame, then insert a copy of the proclamation. As a group, read over and discuss the proclamation.

To Save You Time

Find the proclamation online at www.ldscatalog.com

Gratitude Journals

What You Will Need

- Composition notebooks, plain notebooks (medium size), or binders
- Materials for decorating notebooks or binders (markers, paper, glue dots, scissors, foam shapes, or whatever you have)

What to Do

Give each girl her own notebook. Have girls decorate their notebooks. While they are decorating them or after they finish, talk to them about the importance of gratitude. Have the girls write their first journal entry during the activity. Encourage the girls to write in their journals daily.

Variations

- Give the girls several blank strips of paper. Have them write a question on each one and then put the strips in a box. (Or give them the already-prepared questions and have them cut them into strips to put in their box.) Girls can write in their journals every day at home by simply choosing a question from the box and answering it.
- Tell girls that when they are home, as a memory comes to mind, they should write a quick note on a strip of paper and put it in the jar. When a girl sits down to write in her journal, she can take a strip out of the jar and write a more detailed account of the memory and include it in her journal.

To Save You Time

What is your favorite scripture and why?
What are your favorite family holiday traditions?
Describe your favorite summer activities.
Describe your favorite winter activities.
What's your best Christmas memory?
If you could live anywhere, where would it be? Why?
What are your goals and dreams?
What would you do with a million dollars?
What would be your ultimate birthday or Christmas gift?

Temple Reminder Craft

What You Will Need

- Ceramic tile for each girl (6 x 6 inch works well, but you can use any size of tile)
- Picture of temple printed on regular paper with this sentence typed above the picture: "I will prepare now to marry in the temple." (Print temple and words as one page that will fit on tile. You can print the temple in color or black and white, or use an antiqued effect.)
- Mod Podge®
- Craft brushes
- Popsicle sticks

What to Do

Talk about the importance of preparing now to go to the temple, and the importance of keeping your temple covenants after you have gone through the temple. Sing "I Love to See the Temple."

Give each girl a tile, the temple picture, a foam brush, a popsicle stick, and a small plate of Mod Podge. Have the girls spread a thin layer of Mod Podge onto the tile, then quickly and carefully put the temple picture on the tile. Tell girls to use popsicle sticks to smooth out the wrinkles on the paper. Let Mod Podge dry for a few minutes, then apply another coat over top of temple. Let it dry and repeat a few more times. For this activity, serve temple-shaped sugar cookies, frosted with thin white frosting (royal icing works well) and decorated with candy pearls.

Variations

- Give each girl some marshmallows and toothpicks. Have the girls use their creativity to make temples out of the marshmallows.
- If you have a temple nearby, take the girls on a tour of the temple grounds. Make sure you visit the visitors center if the temple has one. If you call ahead, you may be able to have someone from the temple

presidency talk to the girls. After you arrive at the temple grounds, find a quite spot and talk about the importance of the temple and the ordinances performed inside. Talk about worthiness and always choosing the right. Take a picture of each girl in front of the temple. If possible frame the pictures and bring them to your next activity.

Missionary Lesson

What to Do

Arrange for the missionaries in your area (or a returned missionary) to attend an Activity Day activity and tell the girls what it is like to serve a mission. Have the girls come prepared with questions. Challenge the girls to be a missionary to their friends. Encourage girls to invite nonmember or less-active friends to Primary, Primary activities, or an Activity Day activity. Have girls share their experience at the next activity.

Variations

- Give each girl a Book of Mormon and have her write her testimony in it. Then challenge girls to give the book to someone.
- Have girls role-play how they can share the gospel in conversation, and how they can invite a friend to come with them to church or Primary, or attend family home evening in their home. Explain how sometimes we're afraid to share the gospel. Read 2 Timothy 1:7. Tell girls if they truly love their friends, they'll want to share the gospel with them. If we genuinely want to be a friend, people will sense that and won't be offended when we talk about the Church. In a few weeks, have girls report back any missionary experiences they had.

Testimony Builder

What to Do

Talk about what a testimony is and what is appropriate to say when you bear your testimony. Read a few scriptures about testimonies. Bear your testimony, and encourage the girls to bear theirs. Challenge them to bear their testimonies at the next fast and testimony meeting.

Sacrament Time*

What You Will Need

- Recipe and ingredients for bread (or purchase frozen bread dough)
- Short lesson about the sacrament

What to Do

Teach girls that as we partake of the sacrament with a prayerful and repentant attitude, we renew our baptismal covenants. Teach them about the symbolism of the sacrament—what the bread and water symbolize. Have the girls make bread and give it to the priests to use for the sacrament. (Make sure you get the approval from your bishop.)

Variation

Make the bread and give it to neighbors or people in your ward.

*Also counts as goal in Developing Talents and Serving Others.

It Is "A-Mazing" When We Choose the Right

What You Will Need

- Chairs to create a maze
- Cards with different scenarios, such as "You paid your tithing," "You made the right choice," etc.

What to Do

Set up chairs to create a maze. Girls walk through and go to different tables to draw a card out of a box. If a girl picks a card that says, for example, "You remembered to pay your tithing," she goes the easy way in the maze and gets a card at the end that says something like, "Congratulations. The choices you have made along this path have led you to a temple marriage." If she makes a wrong choice, she has to go a longer, more complicated way.

Learn about Tithing

What You Will Need

- Brief lesson on tithing
- Materials to make a tithing bank (small glass jar, small box, or small, disposable plastic container)
- Materials to decorate bank (foam letters or shapes, glue, permanent markers, scrap paper, etc.)

What to Do

Teach about the importance of paying tithing. Then have the girls make a tithing box or bottle.

Money Management

What You Will Need

- Tips on managing money
- Tithing envelope for each girl
- Monopoly or other play money (can make your own)

Teach the girls the importance of managing their money. Give the girls a certain amount of play money and have them divide it up using this concept. Provide the girls with tithing slips and envelopes, and make sure they understand how to fill out the slips.

To Save You Time

www.pta.org/money_management_for_kids.htm

Variations

- Have a financial planner or other expert teach the class.

- Locate a bank that will take you and the girls on a tour. Ask the manager to talk about deposits, withdrawals, and safety deposit boxes. Have him or her explain how to open an account and why people use a bank instead of just keeping their money at home. If possible, have the manager show you the vault.

Prayer Rock

What You Will Need

- Rock for each girl
- Materials to decorate rock, such as googly eyes, yarn, glue, markers, etc.

What to Do

Prepare a simple lesson on the importance of prayer. Give each girl a rock and have her decorate it. Give each girl a copy of the prayer rock poem. Find one on the internet or use the one below.

Variation

Put the rocks in a 250ºF oven until they are warm but not hot. Give the girls the rocks right out of the oven while they are still warm. Have them use the crayons to draw designs and patterns on the rocks. The crayon should melt on the rocks, giving them a tie-dyed look.

To Save You Time

Prayer Rock Poem

If you get quickly into your warm bed
And feel this rock hit your head
Kneel down and fold your arms to pray,
And thank Heavenly Father for your day.
Ask him for help in everything you do
And know how much he loves you.

Friend Day

What You Will Need

- Depends on what activities you choose (see below)

What to Do

Center an entire activity around the *Friend* magazine. For example, read a story out of the *Friend,* make a craft, do a puzzle, and make a treat using a recipe out of the *Friend.* Have a few issues of the *Friend* for the girls to look at. If girls have a *Friend* subscription, encourage them to read the magazine each month. If not, encourage them to get a subscription if possible. Otherwise, they can read the *Friend* online, or you can offer to share your copy with them.

To Save You Time

Go to lds.org and click on "Search Gospel Library." Go to "Magazines," then click on "Friend. " Select "Print Activities," "Activities Archive," "Find Children's Music," etc. Or go to lds.org, click on "Menu," and look under the section "Family."

Gospel Game on a Giant Game Board

What You Will Need

- Colored tape or colored cardstock
- Large foam dice (or square blocks and markers)
- Index cards with gospel-related questions

What to Do

Make a giant (life-size) game board. Here are a couple of ways to accomplish this: Clear out all the chairs in the room. Using colored masking or duct tape, make squares on the floor. Or laminate colored cardstock and secure it on the floor with duct tape. Leave some of the squares blank, and put instructions on some of them. (Print instructions on the colored cardstock.) Decide what instruction corresponds with what color of square. For example, if a girl lands on a blue square, she will pick a blue card or recite her favorite Article of Faith. If she lands on a red space, she will pick a red card or sing a Primary song. Color-code questions on cards (e.g., blue: Book of Mormon question; red: Article of Faith question, etc.). For dice: Buy foam dice at a novelty store, or use square blocks and draw numbers on with markers.

Faith-in-God Scavenger Hunt

What You Will Need

- *Faith in God for Girls* (book)

What to Do

Write down some questions the girls can find in their *Faith in God* book. Then divide the girls into teams or let them play individually. Have the girls search the book to find the answers.

To Save You Time

Which scripture is on developing talents?

What is the last line of the baptismal covenant? (page 3)

In the section "Developing Talents," what is something you can write that teaches a principle of the gospel?

Name four things Heavenly Father has given you to help you here on earth. (page 1)

We encourage you to ________ and ________the gospel, ________ others, and use the ________Heavenly Father has given you to ___________ and do many ____________." (page 1)

Name three things you covenanted to do when you were baptized. (pages 2–3)

What happens when you repent? (page 2)

What happens when you keep your baptismal covenant? (page 2)

We should _________daily to Heavenly Father.

Read the ___________regularly. (page 4)

How many Articles of Faith are there? _____________

What can you do when you make a mistake? (back cover)

What things will you do on the Sabbath day? (back cover)
What will you not partake of? (back cover)
What kind of music will you listen to? (back cover)
When will you live worthy to go to the temple? (back cover)
In the section "Preparing for Young Women," what Article of Faith should you study?
How many times can you find the word "good" in the section "Developing Talents"?
What two scriptures are found in the section "Serving Others"?
What song will you learn in the section "Learning and Living the Gospel"?

Family Home Evening "Workshop"

What You Will Need

- Items for Each Station:
  - Station 1: Find a flannel-board story from the *Friend* and copy the pictures onto cardstock.
  - Station 2: Sing some Primary songs; make visual aids for a song.
  - Station 3: Print a game from the *Friend* on cardstock. Have girls cut out game. If possible, laminate the game.
  - Station 4: Learn to make simple refreshments for family home evening. Give the girls a copy of the recipe.

What to Do

At the beginning of this activity, talk to the girls about the importance of family home evening. Divide the girls into groups and have them rotate through the activities. Provide zip-top bags to store all their pieces for the games and stories.

Variations

- Don't rotate; just do a couple of activities at different Activity Days. Add new items to kit at other activities.

- Make a family home evening responsibility chart. Leave spaces to fill in who will say the prayer, read a scripture, give the lesson, lead the song, and prepare refreshments.

To Save You Time

Go to lds.org and click on "Search Gospel Library." Go to "Magazines," then click on "Friend. " Select "Print Activities," "Activities Archive," "Find Children's Music," etc. Or go lds.org, click on "Menu," and look under the section "Family."

Make a "Mormon Ad"

What You Will Need

- Several Mormon Ads (found in the *New Era*), from Church Distribution or online
- Paper
- Pencils
- Colored pencils

What to Do

Show the girls the Mormon Ads. After they have studied them for a bit, have them make their own.

Variations

- Assign each girl a gospel topic to make a commercial with, or let girls come up with their own gospel topic. Have them prepare scripts, design costumes, plan props, and then practice their commercials a few times. Then have them present their commercials.
- Make color copies of all the girls' ads. Laminate them or put them in sheet protectors. Buy inexpensive binders and make a book for each girl that includes a copy of every girls' "Mormon ads."

Project Runway—in a Modest Way

What You Will Need

- Scraps of fabric, garbage bags, paper, tinfoil, empty egg cartoons, ribbon, scissors, wrapping paper, tape, and anything else creative you want to bring

What to Do

Divide girls into two teams. Have each team pick one girl to be the "model." The other girls on the team make a modest, creative outfit for their model, over her own clothes. Designers should write up a description of their model's outfit. Have a mini fashion show. Have one girl from each team read the description of their model's outfit as she walks down the "runway." If you have time, have the girls take turns being the model.

Importance of Inspirational Music

What You Will Need

- Church music to play for the girls
- CD player or mp3 player with speakers
- In advance, ask girls to bring their favorite music (be sure to specify whether you need it on a CD or as mp3 files)

What to Do

Talk about how music can invite the Holy Ghost or drive it away. Play the CDs or music files the girls have brought, and let them dance to the music. Talk about the feelings they get when they listen to different types of music. Play or sing the Church songs and notice how they bring different feelings than the other music. Have each girl tell you her favorite Church song. Challenge the girls to be aware of what they are listening to and to turn it off if it does not invite the Spirit.

To Save You Time

http://lds.org/churchmusic/

Choosing Righteous Media

What to Do

Talk to the girls about how we should use the prophets' guidelines (and the Spirit!) to choose media that is uplifting rather than degrading. Play a game to emphasize this. Have a girl say something (like "soap opera") and the other girls say if that's good to watch (or read) or not. The girls can use thumbs up or thumbs down or shout out. Or you can have girls secretly vote for each item and then you read the results. After the game, have the girls discuss what they learned. Ask the girls, "What are some things we shouldn't watch, read, or listen to?" Go around the group and have girls name things.

Gossip Game

What You Will Need

- Brief lesson on gossip

What to Do

Play the gossip game, otherwise known as "telephone." Ask the girls to sit in a circle. One girl whispers a brief sentence about something in the news or anything they want (as long as it is clean and isn't hurtful to anyone) to the next girl, who whispers it to the second, etc. Each girl only whispers the sentence once, not repeating it even if the listening girl asks. The last girl to hear the news states it out loud to the entire group. The girls will be surprised how the sentence has changed from the original.

Explain what gossip is and how it travels quickly. Emphasize that we must watch what we say to others, and that if we hear gossip we shouldn't pass it on. Often what we hear about others isn't true anyway because it has been changed when it was told to someone else, just like it did in the game. (And even if something is true, if it is negative, we shouldn't repeat it unless not doing so could put us or others in danger.)

Read quote from President Spencer W. Kimball: "Lies and gossip which harm reputations are scattered about by the four winds like the seeds of a ripe dandelion held aloft by a child. Neither the seeds nor the gossip can ever be gathered in. The degree and extent of the harm done by the gossip is inestimable" (Spencer W. Kimball, *Miracle of Forgiveness* [Salt Lake City: Deseret Book Co, 1969], 54). Read Proverbs 10:18–19: "He that hideth hatred with lying lips, and he that uttereth a slander, is a fool. In the multitude of words there wanteth not sin: but he that refraineth his lips is wise."

Goal Setting

What You Will Need

- Nice paper for girls to write their goals on
- Short lesson about goal setting (prepare lesson in advance)

What to Do

Present lesson on goals. Explain how to set goals and how to achieve them. Have the girls write down goals they would like to achieve as they grow up. Have the girls write these goals in their best handwriting on the nice paper you have provided. They can hang the list of goals on their bedroom wall, so they can regularly review the goals.

Variation

Have the girls write their goals on a plain piece of paper. Type up their goals on nice paper and bring them to the next Activity Day activity. Laminate or frame the list of goals for more durability.

Nutritious Eating

What You Will Need

- Handouts on healthy eating
- USDA food pyramid
- Healthy refreshments
- Pictures of healthy and unhealthy foods

Teach the girls that if we eat good foods and keep our bodies healthy, we can live longer, be happier, and feel good so we can serve others and want to be obedient to the commandments. Tell girls that the perfect diet is found in the scriptures (Doctrine and Covenants 89). It is called the Word of Wisdom. It tells us what we should and shouldn't eat. Hold up different pictures of foods and ask girls to say if they are healthy or unhealthy, e.g., potato chips (bad!), carrot sticks (good!). Have girls shout out healthy and unhealthy foods. Explain how we can have "junk food" occasionally, but that if we eat it often, our bodies may become diseased and we may not be able to do all the things we love to do. Serve healthy refreshments, like cut-up raw fruit and vegetables. (Review the food pyramid if it goes along with the Word of Wisdom.) Have the girls keep a food journal for three days, balancing what they eat using the food pyramid. Have them report back at your next activity.

Variation*

Each girl plans the meals for her family for one day, trying to use foods from at least three of the food groups (see the food pyramid). Girls go home and help fix a meal for their families. Girls help set the table, cook the food, and wash the dishes.

To Save You Time

www.mypyramid.gov/pyramid/index.html
www.foodnetwork.com/healthy-eating/index.html
http://www.nourishinteractive.com/ (check out the free printables)

*Also passes off goal in Serving Others.

Exercise Day*

What You Will Need

- Balance balls
- Hand weights
- Yoga mats
- Music

Talk about different ways to exercise, and the importance of keeping active. Show girls some different exercises they can do. If needed, bring in an expert.

* Also passes off goal in Developing Talents.

Visit a Nursing Home

What to Do

With the girls, visit a nursing home or care center and talk with the residents about the "good old days." Ask residents which events they remember most, the type of dances they did, who their favorite singers were, etc. Later, help the girls research these events and people, finding as many pictures as you can.

Variations

- Take pictures of residents at a nursing home. On another Activity Day, compile pictures and what you have learned from the residents into a poster or scrapbook. Bring the finished project back to the residents for all of them to enjoy.
- Have the girls make cute stationery with matching envelopes and bookmarks and have them bring it to the nursing home.
- Look up ideas on craft-store websites. Spend one Activity Day making the jewelry. Then spend another activity delivering it to a local nursing home. Or arrange ahead of time to bring the materials (to make necklaces, pins, and tie tacks) to the nursing home. Help the residents make their own jewelry.

To Save You Time

http://robertscrafts.com/default.aspx?PageID=213&ProjectID=206
http://www.joann.com/static/project/0906/P190227_faith_floss_bracelet.pdf

Service for the Elderly

What to Do

Find a service the girls can do for an elderly person or someone else in your neighborhood (for example, raking leaves, vacuuming, or grocery shopping). After the girls perform the service, have them sit down and visit with the person for a while. Often, the elderly (or other people who are ill or shut in) just need someone to talk to.

Breakfast or Lunch with Older Single Sisters

What You Will Need

- Ingredients for a simple breakfast or lunch

What to Do

Have the girls arrive early to set the tables and decorate the room. It would be fun to decorate the room in a theme that matches the era the elderly sisters grew up in. Find old pictures online or in magazines. Pair up girls with elderly sisters. Preferably, they're one-on-one at small tables. In advance, give girls lists of questions they can ask their "sisters," such as, "What games did you like to play when you were my age?" and "What did your mother make you do that you didn't like?"

Feed the Homeless

What You Will Need

- Food for sack lunches (see if your ward will donate the food)

What to Do

Several weeks in advance, call your local homeless shelter to ask if you can bring sack lunches to the shelter. Get the details and requirements for that particular shelter. Have the girls make the sack lunches at Activity Day. If possible, go as a group to the shelter to deliver them.

Springtime Caroling

What You Will Need

- Springtime songs to sing (practice them ahead of time)
- Fresh flowers to present to each person you carol to (check for allergies and maybe bring a silk flower instead)

What to Do

Go to the homes of elderly people in your neighborhood, or whomever you think may need a little company or cheering up. Sing to them and then present them with a fresh flower.

To Save You Time

Springtime Songs: "Springtime Is Coming," "I Often Go Walking," "Whenever I Hear," "Purple Pansies"

Service for Your City

What You Will Need

- Flowers to plant (optional)

What to Do

In advance, call your local Parks and Recreation Department and ask if you can get a tour of City Hall or whatever building houses your city's offices. Ask if there is a service you could do for the city, such as planting flowers around a building or at a park (the city may provide the flowers for you). After the tour of the building, do the service project.

Frozen Meals

What You Will Need

- Ingredients for freezer meals (send around a sign-up sheet at Relief Society to explain what you are doing and to ask for donations)

- Disposable foil pans
- Aluminum foil or plastic wrap
- Zip-top freezer bags
- Permanent marker (to write contents and date on packages)

What to Do

Decide on a main dish that would be quick and easy to make. Have the girls work together to make the dish. After it cools, divide the food equally into several gallon-size zip-top bags or disposable foil pans. Label the packages with what is inside (such as "beef stroganoff"), then add the date and cooking instructions. (If cooking instructions are lengthy, you will need to type them up on a sheet of paper in advance.) While food is cooling, have the girls make cards for a few ill or elderly people (or new mothers) in your ward or neighborhood. Help girls deliver the food and cards. Make sure you ask about food allergies in advance.

Service Scavenger Hunt

What You Will Need

- A list of services for each team to perform for a neighbor or ward member (for example, sweep or vacuum floors, wash dishes, read a story to a child)

What to Do

Divide the girls into two teams. Make sure you have an extra adult to supervise one of the teams. Give each team the list of service projects that you prepared ahead of time. Then have each team go door-to-door (only to houses of ward members or people they know) and ask if they can perform one of the services on the list. The girls on each team work together to accomplish the task. Give them a certain amount of time to finish as many items as they can. Have the two teams meet back at the church. See who finished the most items on their list, but declare both teams the winner, since they all performed acts of service. Serve the girls ice cream or some other sweet treat, because "service is sweet."

Variation

Instead of doing service for people in the neighborhood, have girls race to clean your ward meetinghouse. The object of the game is to see which team can earn the most points while cleaning the meetinghouse. Divide the girls into teams. Each team is assigned an adult to keep track of points. Give each team a list of the jobs with their point values (for example: scrub bathroom toilets—20 points each; vacuum classrooms—5 points for each room; etc.). Give girls a few minutes to look over the list to decide what they want to do. Make sure girls know which cleaning supplies to use for each job, and where the cleaning supplies are located. Provide a prize or treat for both teams, and explain that they are all winners because they did a great job cleaning the Lord's house.

Church Humanitarian Project: Love Bear

What You Will Need

- Fleece
- Stuffing (use quilt batting)
- Pom-poms
- Felt
- Matching thread

What to Do

Go to the LDS Philanthropies website (http://www.ldsphilanthropies.org/) and follow the link below to find instructions for the "Love Bear." Depending on the age of your girls, decide what they can do to help. (At the very least, you will need to sew the bear yourself in advance.) For example, the girls might be able to stuff the bears, cut out felt pieces, hand-sew felt and pom-poms, and/or sew up the hole after stuffing the bear. This website has great ideas for other humanitarian projects that you can do in addition to (or instead of) the Love Bear.

To Save You Time

Links to Love Bear Instructions and Other Humanitarian Projects:
www.ldsphilanthropies.org/humanitarian-services/patterns/easy-bear-3.pdf
www.providentliving.org/content/display/0,11666,4598-1-3263-1,00.html
www.ldsphilanthropies.org/humanitarian-services/humanitarian-pattern.html
http://ce.byu.edu/cw/womensconference/archive/service_project.cfm

Variation

Make a quilt for a local hospital. Give each girl at least one fabric square. Have girls use fabric crayons or markers to decorate the squares in a fun and colorful way. Sew or have someone else sew the quilt together. If possible, take the girls with you to deliver the quilt. (See http://www.projectlinus.org/ or http://www.ldsphilanthropies.org/humanitarian-services/patterns/quilts.pdf.)

Serving Temple Workers and Patrons

What You Will Need

- Cleaning supplies (to clean car windows)
- Copy of note to leave on windows

What to Do

Take a field trip to the temple. Walk around and admire the beautiful temple grounds. Talk about the kind of service we do in the temple, and the service the temple workers do. Tell the girls you will now give them all an opportunity to give service back to the temple patrons and workers. Split up into groups (make sure you have a leader for every group) and wash the windshields of the cars in the temple parking lot. Leave a thank-you note on each car for the patron or temple worker. You might say something like, "Thank you for your service. We hope we helped you see more clearly as you drive home."

Teacher Seed Packets

What You Will Need

- Packets of seeds (can make pretend seed packets and fill them with candy, or empty real seed packets and fill them with candy, but make sure it's a type of seed that won't make the candy taste bad)
- Poem below, printed on nice paper

What to Do

Have the girls attach the following poem to a seed packet and give one to each Primary teacher to thank them for all they do.

Poem

Children are like seeds you nurture to be
Wonderful people in society.

Teachers are patient and loving, as we can see,
Watching us become the best we can be.

Thanks for being such an amazing teacher,
For helping us grow,
And teaching us all that we must know.

Variation

Have the girls give a seed packet and poem to their schoolteachers.

Letter-Writing Party

What You Will Need

- Paper (preferably nice stationery)
- Envelopes
- Pens
- Stamps (optional)

What to Do

Assign each girl to bring the name and address of two relatives or friends that don't live close by. Have girls write letters to these people. Teach the girls the importance of staying in touch with friends and family, and letting them know what's going on in your life and how much you love and miss them. Let the girls know that emails are fine, but there is something special about receiving a letter in the mail.

Variations

- Have girls write letters of encouragement to individuals in your ward or neighborhood that might need a little pick-me-up. After reading over the letters, mail them to the individuals.
- Organize a card drive in your ward for the Ronald McDonald House, or have an activity where the girls make cards to donate. The Ronald McDonald Houses are always in need of cards to give to the families of sick children.
- Randomly send postcards to your Activity Day girls. On each postcard, write a note of praise and encouragement. Include a spiritual thought. Send postcards to less-active girls on a regular basis, letting them know you missed seeing them. Mail or drop off a monthly calendar of activities to your less-active girls.

Make Thank-You Cards*

What You Will Need

- Materials to make cards—old cards, cardstock, scrapbooking supplies, ribbon, envelopes, etc.
- Pens
- Brief lesson on gratitude.

What to Do

Teach lesson on gratitude and the importance of being thankful for everything we have. Tell the story of the ten lepers (see Luke 17:11–19). Emphasize the importance of giving thanks in our prayers and telling those around us how thankful we are for the things they do for us. Have each girl make a variety of greeting cards and write a thank-you note to a parent, teacher, sibling, friend, or teacher.

Variation

Write thank-you notes to your local firefighters or police officers. Make cookies and attach the thank-you notes to the package. Deliver the treats to your local fire station or police station.

*Also passes off goal in Developing Talents.

Honoring Military Personnel

What You Will Need

- Paper
- Pens

What to Do

Have military personnel or families of military personnel come talk to the girls. Ask them to explain what it is like to serve in the military, or to have a family member who does. If possible, have them bring uniforms, pictures, medals, etc. Tell them the purpose of this activity is to give the girls a better understanding of the sacrifices that military personnel make for their country. Explain to the girls the importance of these men and woman and their service. Have the girls write thank-you notes to the speaker, thanking him or her for his or her military service, or for the service of his or her family member.

Variations

- Have the girls gather items that military personnel may need, and then mail the items to the personnel.
- Make a treat at an activity to mail to military personnel. Make something that won't melt, fall apart, or go bad during shipment. You might try things like peanut brittle, plain popcorn, or candied popcorn.

- Ask military personnel (or their families) what items they would like to receive (things like deodorant, soap, toothbrushes, etc). A few weeks in advance, pass out a flyer in Relief Society, elders quorum, etc., asking ward members to donate the needed items.

Thank-You Candy Poster

What You Will Need

- Poster board and candy

What to Do

Have girls make a candy poster for a person in the ward they would like to thank, such as the bishop or the Primary president. Use candy bars or small bags of candy instead of some of the words. Present the poster to the person and let him or her know how much you appreciate everything he or she does. Can also have girls write individual notes to the person. Deliver the poster, or if you choose the bishop, put it on the door of his office at the meetinghouse.

To Save You Time

Here is a sample poster wording (words in all capital letters should be substituted with the candy of that name).

> Dear Bishop,
> You are a LIFESAVER. Thank you for the MOUNDS of work you do for us. You are an EXTRA special man. You always make us SNICKER with your jokes. You always teach us to CHEWS the right. You are our HERO, and we love you to PIECES [use Reese's Pieces and put a piece of paper over "Reese's"].
>
> Love, the Activity Day girls

Be a Good Friend

What You Will Need

- Strips of paper with ways to be a good friend (for example, invite a friend to Primary, bring a friend to an Activity Day activity, invite a friend to sit by you at lunch, etc.)
- Container to hold strips of paper

What to Do

Tell the girls how important it is to be a good friend to everyone, just as Jesus was. Just saying hello or a kind word to someone can have a huge impact on him or her. Teach girls the golden rule: "Do unto others as you would have them do unto you." (In other words, we should treat others how we would like to be treated.) Explain that girls should treat everyone well, not just their close friends. Encourage girls to do spiritual things (like attending Primary) with friends, especially nonmember friends. Teach girls to be good examples to their friends by living the gospel standards. Take out the strips of paper that give ideas of how we can be a good friend. Discuss each one, then have the girls put the strips in their containers.

Variations

- Bring blank strips of paper, and have the girls write ways they can be a good friend.
- Make treats or small gifts and have the girls take them to the nonmember and inactive girls in your ward. Make sure you continue inviting them to your activities.

Small Change

What You Will Need

- Empty jar for each girl
- Materials to decorate jar
- Ahead of time, read the book *Small Change: The Secret life of Penny Burford*

What to Do

Teach the girls the importance of charity and helping others. (Try to do this activity early in the year so the girls will have plenty of time to save money.) Explain how loose change can add up quickly if we save it, and how that money can be used to help the less fortunate. Talk about Penny Burford's story. Give each girl a small jar to decorate. This will now become their "small change" jar. Every time they (and hopefully all their family members) have loose change, they can put it in the jar. At the end of the year, help the girls use the money to help someone in need. Decide ahead of time whom they can donate to. For example: Sub for Santa, a children's hospital, a woman's shelter, or a homeless shelter.

Feeding the Missionaries*

What You Will Need

- Ingredients to prepare a meal for the missionaries (see if you can get donations from the ward, or have each girl contribute an item)

What to Do

Plan a simple menu to feed the missionaries assigned to your ward. Talk to the missionaries in advance to find out what time they would like dinner delivered. Find out if any of the missionaries have food allergies; if they do, plan the food accordingly. Divide the girls into stations and have each station prepare a different part of the dinner. As a group, take the dinner to the missionaries.

Variations

- Have the girls plan the menu and make a shopping list. Then take them to the store to purchase the food. This is a good opportunity to talk to them about budgeting, nutrition, and the four food groups.
- If you have the time, eat dinner with the missionaries and take the opportunity to ask them questions about their missions.

*Also passes off goal in Developing Talents.

Birthday Party for Missionaries

What You Will Need

- See below (have girls bring items, or ask the ward to donate them)

What to Do

Find out the birthdays of the missionaries assigned to your stake. If there are no local missionaries, find out the birthdays of the missionaries from your ward who are serving in the mission field.

For missionaries out in the field: Have the girls bake cookies, make birthday cards, and write notes about favorite Book of Mormon stories, or write testimonies that could be put in the Books of Mormon the missionaries give out. Help girls make a birthday party kit that includes birthday crowns, streamers, cake mix, canned frosting, napkins, paper plates, cups, candles, and small gifts a missionary might need. Mail the kit to each missionary so it arrives in time for his or her birthday.

For missionaries in your stake: Help the girls plan a birthday party for them. Do the things you would do for missionaries in the field (see above), but have the girls make the cake and decorate it. Invite the bishopric and other ward members to the party.

Variation

Have girls write letters and prepare Christmas care packages to send to missionaries from your ward. You can have the girls make items like cookies, or buy items like stamps, stationery, pens, etc. to put in the packages.

Prepare-to-Be-a-Babysitter Relay Race*

What You Will Need

- Items for relay stations

What to Do

Ahead of time, set up the relay stations. Start the activity with a detailed story about a girl going babysitting and the things she encounters. Include the tasks the girls will need to do when they go to the relay stations. For the relay race, have each girl go to each station to see how fast she can accomplish the tasks.

Household Hazards: Have each girl name the hazards as fast as she can. Open pill bottles (don't use real pills), toys on stairs, pot of water with handle facing out, cleaners left out, cord plugged in and stretched across floor, etc.
Diaper-Changing Station: Clean diaper, wipes, dirty diaper on a baby doll. (Use water or even chocolate syrup for a messy diaper.)
First-Aid Station: Baby doll with a fake scratch (use marker to draw one), antiseptic (to clean "scratch"), bandages.
Answering-Phone Station: Bring a cell phone or regular phone and ask another person to call you on it. Have her pretend to be different people. Good chance to talk about phone etiquette and phone safety. (Never tell them parents aren't home, etc.)

*Also passes off goal in Developing Talents.

Babysitting Bag or Shoebox*

This project will take at least two Activity Days to finish.

What You Will Need

- A tote bag or shoebox for each girl (or ask each girl to bring her own)
- Materials to decorate bag or shoebox (make it fun and bright, since it will be for babysitting)
- Items to fill bag with

What to Do

Help girls put together the following to put in their bags:

First-aid and safety information: Make mini first-aid kits with laminated instructions and emergency numbers.
Developmental information: Include information on what is age-appropriate for babies and toddlers.
Songs and finger plays: Make a CD of children's music and finger plays.
Craft activities: Make play dough, coloring pages, etc.
Healthy snacks: Teach girls about healthy snacks they can make that do not require the use of the stove. Ahead of time, make a handout that has a list of healthy snacks.
Games and activities: Have girls collect various songs, finger plays, stories, games, and any other fun activities to do while babysitting. Write them on individual cards, or type them and then glue them on the cards.

Variation

Have a mini "day care." Have the girls each bring a younger sibling or neighbor. Practice what you learned with the younger children. Or offer a night of free babysitting for parents while they attend a Church-sponsored activity: the temple, a leadership meeting, a fireside, etc.

To Save You Time

http://www.preschoolexpress.com/
http://familyfun.go.com/
http://www.kaboose.com/

*Also passes off goal in Developing Talents.

Make a Quiet Book for Younger Children

What You Will Need

- Fabric
- Fabric markers

- Velcro
- Foam embellishments (to use for shapes on book)

What to Do

Have the girls make a fabric quiet book for younger children. Have pages where children can match up colors, shapes, animals, etc. Could also laminate pictures the girls find on the internet or in magazines. The girls can donate the books to the ward nursery, give them to younger siblings, or keep them for their babysitting kit.

Variation

Make a file-folder game. The file folder itself, opened up, is the game board. The game pieces can be placed in a pocket on the back of the folder.

To Save You Time

http://quietbook.blogspot.com/
http://www.ldsphilanthropies.org/humanitarian-services/patterns/fabric-activity-book.pdf

Make an I-Spy Bag for Nursery

What You Will Need

- Fabric or felt
- Rice or poly-fill beads
- Transparent vinyl (available at fabric store)
- Trinkets to put in bag

What to Do

Make I-spy bags and donate them to the ward nursery. Sew the bags ahead of time, leaving a hole on the side so the bag can be filled. (You also need to cut a large hole in the fabric and cover the hole with transparent vinyl so children can see into the bag.) Have girls fill bags with small trinkets (shaped buttons work great), and then rice or beads. Have girls hand-sew the filling hole closed. Have girls present bags to the ward nursery.

Variations

- Donate bags to a homeless shelter, a children's hospital, etc.
- Make other items for the ward nursery (or other organizations), such as file-folder games or homemade puzzles. For homemade puzzles, print pictures from the internet, then laminate them and cut them into puzzle pieces.

To Save You Time

http://www.makeit-loveit.com/2009/02/eye-spy-bags.html
http://blissfullydomestic.com/2008/i-spy-bags
http://ajpadilla.com/reduce-reuse-recycle/i-spy-bag

Reading to a Younger Child

What You Will Need

- Children's books
- *Friend* magazine or scripture stories
- Refreshments

What to Do

At an earlier activity, teach the girls how to read to someone—show pictures, read loudly, make funny voices if needed, use expression in their voices, etc. Have girls practice. Then have each girl bring a younger child (sibling, neighbor, or cousin) to the next activity. Have each girl find a quiet spot to quietly read to the younger child she brought. Have them enjoy refreshments after or during the reading time.

Variation

Using a tape player, have the girls record their voices reading a children's book. Then donate the recording to a local children's hospital, a homeless shelter, a women's shelter, or a nursery.

Be Prepared*

What You Will Need

- Handouts on basic first aid
- Ask a nurse in your ward to come teach the girls (optional)

What to Do

Have a local paramedic or EMT teach the basics of CPR and rescue breathing, or take a field trip to the local fire station. Teach the girls the basics for first aid—how to stop bleeding; what to do if someone is choking; what to do for bites, burns, poisoning, etc. Explain what girls need to do in an emergency (when to call 911, etc.). Explain how to treat minor injuries, how to know when you should go to the doctor, how to avoid spreading colds and flu, etc. (Look at Scouting manuals or girls' camp books for ideas). Teach the girls how the prophets have commanded us to be to be prepared for emergencies, natural disasters, and times when our family doesn't have income. Read the latter part of Doctrine and Covenants 38:30: "If ye are prepared ye shall not fear."

Variation

Accident preparedness: Have an expert (doctor, nurse, EMT, or firefighter) explain what to do if you or someone else is in an accident (car, boat, school bus). For example: Don't move anyone who is seriously injured, and stay out of street.

To Save You Time

http://www.cyh.com/HealthTopics/HealthTopicDetailsKids.aspx?p=335&id=1567&np=285

http://life.familyeducation.com/activity/first-aid/39517.html

*Also passes off goal in Developing Talents.

Family Favorites Cookbook

What You Will Need

- Recipes (have girls bring them)
- Paper (to make cover for the book)
- Markers
- Colored pencils
- Hole punch
- Ribbon or binders (see "What to Do")

What to Do

Have each girl bring a copy of at least two family recipes. Have the girls decorate covers for the recipe book, then help them bind the recipes together to make a book. (Could punch holes in the recipes and the cover and then tie together with ribbon, or punch holes in the recipes and put them in a binder with the cover decorated.) Have the girls tell why they like each recipe, and if there is anything special about their recipes. Have each girl bring a food sample to share. Each girl can give the recipe book to her mother for Mother's Day.

Create a Family Newsletter

What You Will Need

- Paper
- Pens, markers, or colored pencils

What to Do

Ahead of time, ask girls to gather information about their family for a newsletter. (This can include extended family.) You might have them include things like upcoming birthdays, accomplishments, upcoming activities, parties, baseball games, tryouts, etc. Have girls bring their ideas and write up their newsletter. Alternately, girls can type the newsletter at home and bring it to Activity Day. Make copies for girls to give their relatives

Variation

Have the girls make an Activity Day newsletter. Give each girl an assignment (for example, favorite scripture story, comics, upcoming activities, accomplishments of girls).

Family Calendar

What You Will Need

- 12 blank monthly calendars or 1 blank yearly calendar
- Colored pencils or markers
- Stickers for birthdays or other special occasions (optional)

What to Do

Have the girls make a calendar for of all the birthdays and wedding anniversaries in their family. Make copies and have the girls share them with their relatives.

Stories for Grandparents

What You Will Need

- Paper to write stories on

What to Do

Have each girl interview a grandparent (their own or one in the ward or neighborhood). Have the girl ask the grandparent several questions to get them telling stories. (See examples under "To Save You Time.") Then have the girls neatly write or type the questions and answers. Put them in a book or binder and have the girls give them to the grandparents.

To Save You Time

What was your favorite game to play?
How much did a burger cost when you were in elementary school?
What was your favorite subject in school?
What was your favorite toy?

Did you have a TV? If so, what was your favorite show?
Tell me some stories from your childhood.
What did you do for a living?

Family Home Evening about the First Vision*

What You Will Need

- Materials to create visual aids for family home evening kit (find information online)
- Zip-top bags or file folders
- A brief lesson on the First Vision

What to Do

Present a simple lesson on the First Vision to make sure girls know the story. Have the girls make simple family home evening kits. Have them use pictures you found ahead of time as visual aids, or girls can draw their own. Laminate pictures for durability. Provide girls with zip-top bags or file folders with sides taped, to hold everything together in one place. Have girls go home and present the family home evening to their families. At the next activity, have girls report their experiences. See the July 2001 *Friend* for more ideas.

Variations

- Use any gospel standard or scripture story for the family home evening.
- Have each girl make a simple family home evening chart. It should include the different assignments for each family member: song, scripture, lesson, treat, or prayer.

To Save You Time

www.josephsmith.net/
http://lds.org/images/Magazines/Friend/Archive/fr08may48_joseph.jpg
http://lds.org/images/Magazines/Friend/Archive/fr08jun48_joseph.jpg

*Also passes off goal in Learning and Living the Gospel.

Chore Chart

What You Will Need

- Chore charts for girls to personalize and decorate

What to Do

Help the girls understand the importance of helping around the house. Talk about chores the girls can do at home, and chores that other family members do. Hand out the chore charts, which list which chores each family member will do. Have the girls personalize and decorate their charts. At your next activity, have the girls report how they did.

Variation

Make a job jar. Give each girl a quart jar with cloth on the lid. Provide the girls with blank strips of paper. On the strips of paper, have the girls write jobs they can do to help around the house. (Some of these jobs should be things they aren't regularly assigned to do at home.) Then the girls put the strips of paper in the jar and take it home. Challenge girls to do at least one job a day from the jar.

To Save You Time

http://familyfun.go.com/printables/chore-chart-702875/

Saving Energy

What You Will Need

- Handout that lists ideas for saving energy

What to Do

Teach girls how to save energy in their homes. Examples: turning off lights and appliances when not in use; unplugging small appliances (such as toasters) and Ipod or cell-phone chargers when not in use; taking shorter showers to use less hot water; hanging clothes to dry straight from washer, or placing them in dryer just long enough to remove wrinkles, then hanging them; keeping thermostat low in the winter and high in the summer.

To Save You Time

http://www.energyquest.ca.gov/saving_energy/index.html
http://www.eere.energy.gov/kids/games.html
http://www.energystar.gov/index.cfm?c=kids.kids_index

Recycle and Reuse for a Better Life

What You Will Need

- Information about recycling in your area
- Handouts about recyling to give to girls

What to Do

Teach girls about how important it is to take care of the earth that the Savior and our Heavenly Father have created for us. Recycling and reusing helps us reduce waste and pollution. Show examples of the kinds of things that can be recycled or reused. Ask girls to save recyclable items for a month, and then take them to a recycling center together (or use your city's recycling service).

To Save You Time

http://www.energyquest.ca.gov/saving_energy RECYCLINGFactsGames Crafts02.PDF
http://kids.niehs.nih.gov/recycle.htm

Table Manners*

What You Will Need

- Full place setting

What to Do

Talk about table manners. Show the girls how to set a formal and informal place setting at the table. Teach them what each utensil is for, how to use a napkin, etc. Have girls take turns practicing which utensil to use and how to set the table.

Variations

- Send a handout home with the girls.
- Teach the girls good manners (in general) and courtesy, in addition to table manners. Find a book on manners Teach girls phone etiquette, how and when to write a thank-you note, and how to speak to and answer someone correctly. Have girls practice what they have learned.

To Save You Time

http://www.drdaveanddee.com/elbows.html

http://home.centurytel.net/mrs_browns_classroom/pages/manners.htm

*Also passes off goal in Developing Talents.

What's Cooking?

What You Will Need

- Ingredients to make a simple food item

What to Do

Teach girls basic cooking skills. For an activity, have girls make cookies and take them to a friend. Make snacks for activity—popcorn, cut-up vegetables, etc. Make trail food for a hike. Make a dessert for your family (JELL-O, brownies, pudding, s'mores, or pigs in blankets).

Variation

Teach the girls basic cooking skills and how to properly measure ingredients. Also teach them how to substitute certain ingredients to make a dish healthier.

To Save You Time

www.joyofbaking.com/IngredientSubstitution.html

www.nutribase.com/foodsub.shtml

www.health.gov/dietaryguidelines/dga2005/healthieryou/html/tips_healthy_subs.html

Party Planning*

What You Will Need

- Items to make invitations

What to Do

Have the girls help plan a party. The party can be for a daddy-daughter date or a recognition night. Have girls plan the theme, food, decorations, and any activities. Have the girls make invitations (if short on time, have the girls make the invitations at another activity).

Variation

Have the girls plan and throw a party for younger children, or have the girls help Primary leaders plan and hold a Primary quarterly activity.

Home Depot Workshops

What You Will Need

- Contact a local Home Depot store to make sure they have the free project program

What to Do

Most Home Depot stores offer a free workshop for children ages five to eleven, the first Saturday of every month from 9 a.m. to noon. The store provides all supplies to make the project, which changes each month. Each child gets a project and a child-size apron. Just make sure you get there early in case they run out of space and supplies. Some Home Depot stores let you sign up ahead of time. If you do not have a Home Depot in your area, check with other hardware stores.

Personal Hygiene Kits

What You Will Need

- Items for kit, such as deodorant, loofah, soap, washcloth, lip gloss, hand sanitizer, shampoo, conditioner, headband, tissues, toothbrush, gum, lotion, elastic bands, body spray, nail polish, nail file, nail clippers, comb (use sample-size items if possible)

- Personal hygiene chart to keep track of brushing teeth, washing hair, etc.
- Small, inexpensive makeup bags (purchase at a dollar store)

What to Do

Talk to the girls about the importance of keeping our bodies clean. Make sure the girls know all the things they should do—brush teeth at least twice a day, wash hair often, use deodorant when old enough, etc. To really get your point across, have your Activity Day partner enlist help from a young woman in the ward, or one of your girls' mothers. Have her come in with her hair uncombed, dirty clothes, gross things on her teeth, dirt on face and arms, etc. At first, act like you don't notice. Then act like she smells or has bad breath. Really ham it up, so the girls know you're joking around. Ask her when she last combed her hair, brushed her teeth, changed her clothes, etc. Have her look in a small hand-held mirror and have her act shocked at her appearance. Give her a bag with clean clothes, a hairbrush, a toothbrush, etc. Have her go change, wash up, comb her hair, brush her teeth, and come back looking much better. Discuss with the girls what a big difference it was when she took care of herself. Teach the girls that our body is a temple and we can show respect to it by keeping it clean. (Be careful to not offend anyone or say too much.) Give a personal hygiene kit to each girl. Go through the items, explaining what each is used for. Answer any questions the girls may have.

Create a Piece of Art

What You Will Need

- Items to make something to display (for example, embroidery, cross-stitch, or water color)

What to Do

Teach the girls how to make a craft or art item. After they have completed their project, plan a night for them to display their art and have their parents and others come to the "show."

Variation

Have a short lesson about a famous artist. Then have the girls do an art project that uses the famous artist's techniques. Have a night where the girls can display their art pieces. Put them up around a room in the meetinghouse. Invite parents and whomever else the girls want to come, and have the girls and guests walk around your "art gallery." Serve light refreshments.

Write a Play*

What You Will Need

- Various items to use as props, scenery, and sound effects

What to Do

Have the girls write a play that teaches a gospel principle or teaches about Heavenly Father's creations. Make costumes, scenery, and sound effects. Girls can perform the play for parents at an Activity Day social.

*Also passes off goal for Learning and Living the Gospel.

Write a Poem

What You Will Need

- Brief lesson about different forms of poetry
- Paper
- Pen

What to Do

Teach the girls about different kinds of poems. Show girls a few sample poems, then have each girl write a few poems. Have girls take turns sharing their poems. Bind poems in a book for each girl.

Variation

- Have the girls use their best handwriting or calligraphy to write their poems. Put each girl's poem in a simple cardboard frame that she can decorate.

To Save You Time

Cinquain

line 1: one word
line 2: two words
line 3: three words
line 4: four words
line 5: one word

Variations: line 1—one noun, line 2—two adjectives, line 3—three -ing words, line 4—a phrase, line 5—one synonym for the noun; OR line 1—two syllables, line 2—four syllables, line 3—six syllables, line 4—eight syllables, line 5—two syllables.

Haiku

line 1: five syllables
line 2: seven syllables
line 3: five syllables

Shape Poem

Pick a topic to write about. Think about a shape that would go along with the topic. Write the poem neatly around the outline of the shape, OR write the lines so that the body of the poem forms the shape.

Free-Verse Poem

Anything girls want to write, OR rhyming poem.

Band for a Day

What You Will Need

- Musical instruments (have girls bring the ones they play)
- Simple or homemade musical instruments (for girls who don't play a musical instrument)

What to Do

Have the girls write and perform a song, or play something from the hymnbook or the Primary songbook. Talk about the importance of developing our talents and brightening our lives and the lives of others with good music. Read a scripture or General Authority quote about sharing our talents.

Glamour Night

What You Will Need

- Nail polish, nail polish remover, nail decals and glue, etc.
- Hairstyling items
- Large mirror
- Camera (optional)

What to Do

Invite a hairstylist or cosmetology student to come and teach the girls. This might be a fun activity to invite the Young Women to. Teach the girls about skin care, makeup, and hairstyling. Have the Young Women or Activity Days girls help each other paint their nails, try different hairstyles, etc. Explain how we should try to look our best but not focus on that. It is best to make sure we look our best and then forget about ourselves and help others. If we feel good about ourselves, we can serve others better. This activity would work well as a Mother-Daughter date.

Variations

- If possible, set up a large mirror with a small table and a chair in front of it. Take before-and-after photos of each girl. Have a hairstylist or cosmetology student do the girls' hair in dressy styles so they will look dramatically different than they normally do (think crowns, flowers, ribbons, etc.). Take pictures of the girls in their fancy new hairstyles.
- Have your special guest teach the girls all about nail care. She should start with the basics and teach the girls the proper technique for

painting nails and removing nail polish. If you have the supplies, have her teach the girls some fun nail tricks—how to add flowers, dots, etc. Have the girls practice on each other.

Take a Hike

What You Will Need

- Information on simple hikes in your area
- Water bottles and sunscreen (have girls bring)
- List of local plants for each girl (optional)

What to Do

Take the girls on a simple hike. Point out interesting objects, sites, plants etc. If you printed a list of local plants, have the girls find as many on the list as they can. Enjoy the wonderful outdoors!

Variations

- Turn the hike into a scavenger hunt. For each girl or team, make a list of things they might see on the hike. Have the girls find as many items on the list as they can. (If dividing girls in teams, each team needs an adult leader.)
- Make a nature bracelet. Before the hike, place masking tape around each girl's wrist with the sticky side facing away from the skin. Have each girl make a nature bracelet with soil, leaves, flowers, etc., that she finds on the hike.

Powder-Puff Derby

What You Will Need

- Pinewood derby cars (purchase at your local Boy Scout store)

What to Do

Give each girl a pinewood derby car to take home and decorate. Make sure all the girls have someone to help them cut out the car; if not, find someone in the ward that can help them. Make a whole night out of it, just like the Cub Scouts do!

Various Versions of Tag

What You Will Need

- Flashlight for flashlight tag

Regular Tag: One girl is "it." She chases everyone until she touches someone else. Once someone else is touched, she is "it."
Freeze Tag: The girl who is "it" chases everyone. When a girl is tagged, she must remain in her spot ("frozen") until someone who has not been frozen comes to tag her. Once the frozen girl is tagged by a free person, she is also free. The girl who is "it" tries to get everyone frozen.
Walk Tag: Same as regular tag, but the girls walk instead of run.
Flashlight Tag. Turn off all the lights in the church gym. Whoever is "it" gets a flashlight and closes her eyes until everyone has hidden. Once everyone is hidden, "it" turns on the flashlight and goes to find the others. The first person tagged becomes "it." Some people may remain hidden. (Variation: Have everyone wear glow-in-the-dark bracelets or necklaces.)
Everybody's It! Play this the same way you would regular tag, except everybody is "it." Everyone runs around trying to tag everyone else. Once you are tagged you sit down. Last person standing wins.
Cartoon Tag. One girl is "it." If you are about to be tagged you, you need to quickly say the name of a cartoon. If you don't say the name of a cartoon before you are tagged, you become "it."
Colored-Egg Tag. Start the game by picking a wolf and a mother chicken. Everyone else is colored eggs. The wolf leaves the area, and the mother chicken asks all the other eggs what color they want to be. Once the mother chicken finds out the colors of the eggs, she calls the wolf. When the wolf comes up, the mother chicken turns her back to him and faces the eggs. The wolf knocks on the mother chicken's back (like

a door), and the dialog begins. (This dialog is important to playing the game correctly.)

Wolf: Knock, knock!
Mother chicken: Who's there?
Wolf: The big bad wolf.
Mother chicken: What do you want?
Wolf: Colored eggs.
Mother chicken: What color?

The wolf starts picking colors. When one of the egg's colors is picked, that egg gets a three-second head start to run around a designated area without getting tagged (around a tree, bush, fire hydrant, etc.). Even if the player gets tagged, the game continues, until all the eggs have been chosen. The last player to be tagged becomes the wolf, and the wolf of that round becomes the mother chicken. The mother chicken becomes one of the eggs.

Dinner on a Budget

What You Will Need

- Approximately $20 to buy food
- Store ads if using variation

What to Do

Give the girls a budget of about $20. Have them plan a dinner and buy the items to make a full dinner for that amount. Divide girls into four groups. Give each group $5 and a different food category, such as appetizer, fruit, salad or side, main dish, and dessert. Remind girls of any food tax you may have in your area. Give them about fifteen minutes to shop. Then go back to someone's house and prepare the meal.

Variation

Bring a number of store advertisements. Have the girls find the items for their category on the ad. Make sure they stay on budget and remember sales tax if there is any. No need to actually shop or prepare the meal.

Good-Old-Days Games

What You Will Need

- Any items needed to play the games (see "What to Do")

What to Do

In advance, give the girls the assignment to research or ask their parents, an aunt or uncle, or their grandparents about the sports or games they liked to play when they were young. Play some of these games at the next Activity Day. Have old-fashioned treats like root-beer floats.

To Save You Time

Some old-fashioned games include jacks, Steal the Flag, marbles, Red Rover, Charades, Marco Polo, and Hot Potato (see http://en.wikipedia.org/wiki/List_of_traditional_children%27s_games).

Old-Fashioned "Do"

What You Will Need

- Photographs of old-fashioned hairstyles (the internet is a good place to find these)
- Hairstyling tools and accessories (brushes, combs, bobby pins, hairspray, styling gel, etc.)

What to Do

Have the girls see if they can do their hair in some of the styles in the pictures. Have a mini fashion show after.

Variation

Blindfold one girl and have another girl do the craziest hairstyle on the blindfolded person, then switch. Make sure you take pictures.

Face Painting

What You Will Need

- Face paint or other washable, nontoxic paint
- Cotton swabs or small paint brushes
- Paper and pencils (for practicing)
- Pictures from internet (samples of what the girls can draw)

What to Do

Have the girls decide what they want to paint, then practice drawing with paper and pencil before they start painting. After they have mastered drawing the objects or designs, the girls should practice painting on each other or on their own arms. Have them use their new face-painting skills at a Primary activity. Or have a Halloween party and invite some of the Primary kids and paint their faces.

Purse Notebook

What You Will Need

- Composition notebook
- Exacto knife
- Scrapbook paper
- Mod Podge®
- Embellishments
- Ribbon
- Hot glue gun

What to Do

Use an exacto knife to trim the corners off both sides of the notebook (the side that opens up, not the bound side). The notebook should now be the shape of a purse. Do this ahead of time for the girls. At the activity, have the girls cover both sides of the notebook with scrapbook paper, using Mod Podge as glue. After the Mod Podge dries, trim off the excess paper. Hot-glue ribbons on the front and back covers as handles. Hot-glue a piece of ribbon that you can use as a latch to shut purse. Tie the two ribbons together or use sticky-back Velcro. Add embellishments.

Variation

Follow the steps above, but do not trim the corners of the notebook. You will just have a square notebook purse.

CTR or Article of Faith Soap

What You Will Need

- Bar of soap for each girl (inexpensive soap works just fine)
- Copy of CTR shield (sized to fit soap), or copy an Article of Faith (sized to fit soap; may need to split up into two bars of soap)
- Paper
- Wax
- Cellophane bags
- Ribbon
- Note cards, or cardstock to make note cards

What to Do

Print CTR shields on paper. Then have the girls cut them out and put one on each bar of soap. Dip only the front of the soap into the melted wax; this will seal the shield to the soap. Put each bar of soap in a cellophane bag, then tie it closed with a ribbon and attach a cute note.

Variations

- Take the soap to someone that could use a smile. (Also passes off goal in Serving Others.)
- Use any picture on soap. Wrapping paper works great; thicker paper does not work as well.

Family Comic Strip

What You Will Need

- Sample comic strips
- Paper
- Pencils and colored pencils

What to Do

Have each girl think of a funny moment with her family. Show girls what a comic strip looks like, in case they haven't seen or read one before. Have each girl create her own family comic strip.

Make Fun Jewelry

What You Will Need

- Jewelry wire and clasps
- Inexpensive beads (ask girls to bring what they have at home)

What to Do

Show the girls how to make a simple bracelet or necklace (if you have an expert in your ward, invite her to come teach). Have each girl make her own bracelet or necklace. Explain to the girls that Heavenly Father loves them and considers them His jewels (see Malachi 3:17). Tell the girls that when they look at their bracelet or necklace, they can remember how much the Lord loves them.

Variation

Have the girls make the necklaces or bracelets for individuals in your ward (preferably a nonmember or inactive Activity girl). Attach a cute tag with Malachi 3:17 typed out on it.

Magnetic Boards and Clothespin Magnets

What You Will Need

- Sheet metal (buy at hardware stores)
- Picture frames (whatever size you want) without glass
- Scrapbook paper and embellishments
- Mod Podge®
- Clothespins
- Magnets that will fit on back of clothespins

What to Do

Cut sheet metal so it fits into your picture frame. Have the girls decorate the frames by using Mod Podge to cover it with scraps of paper. Add embellishments. When frame is dry, insert sheet metal into frame like you would a picture. To make the magnets, have the girls Mod Podge some pretty paper onto the front of the clothespins. Trim excess paper after it dries. Hot-glue a magnet onto the back of each clothespin. Make sure it is a strong enough magnet to be able to hold the clothespin on a magnetic board and to hold a picture in the clothespin.

Memory Board or Note Board

What You Will Need

- Ribbon
- Thumbtacks
- corkboard
- Piece of fabric to cover foam core (have girls bring)
- Hot glue gun

What to Do

Have the girls glue the piece of fabric onto the corkboard. Have them crisscross the ribbon on the board and secure with thumbtacks. Stick notes, pictures, etc., onto the board under the ribbon.

Architecture

What You Will Need

- Paper (larger than 8½" x 11" works best)
- Pencils
- Colored pencils
- Rulers to make straight lines
- Actual architectural plan or blueprints for a house (optional)

What to Do

Have the girls design their own dream house. Have them include details, label the rooms, etc. Younger girls can make a simple version; older girls can add more details.

Variation

Have the girls go through magazines and find pictures of rooms, furniture, and architecture they like. Have them put pictures together in a book.

Cake Decorating

What You Will Need

- Small cakes (order from bakery or grocery store) or cupcakes (provide for girl or have them bring their own)
- Frosting
- Cake-decorating bags or zip-top plastic bags
- Other cake-decorating supplies

What to Do

Give each girl a small cake or cupcake to decorate. Encourage them to make theirs unique. Afterward, talk to the girls about their individual worth. Ask them if all their cakes are decorated the same. Tell them they are all sweet and beautiful just like their cakes!

Variation

Have someone, such as a professional baker, come and teach the girls how to decorate cakes.

Flip-Flop Fun

What You Will Need

- Flip-flops for each girl (find inexpensive flip-flops at a dollar store or craft store)
- Scraps of fabrics (such as tulle)

What to Do

Tie scraps of fabric onto the straps of the flips-flops to make a fancy, fun flip-flop. You can even tie the fabric into bows or flowers.

Friendship Bracelets

What You Will Need

- Embroidery floss in a variety of colors

What to Do

Make friendship bracelets with embroidery floss. Girls can grab a partner and help each other braid the floss.

To Save You Time

www.wikihow.com/Make-a-Friendship-Bracelet

Flower Headbands

What You Will Need

- Yarn
- Crochet needle for each girl
- Large silk or crocheted flowers
- Needle and thread to sew on flower

What to Do

Teach girls how to crochet a simple headband. Have the girls hand-sew the silk or crocheted flowers onto the headbands. Take a group picture of all the girls wearing their headbands.

Variations

- Buy inexpensive, simple elastic headbands, silk flowers, and faux jewels. Have the girls sew or glue the flowers onto the headbands, then put a jewel in the center of the flowers.
- Have girls make a button headband by gluing a variety of buttons on a stretchy headband. Use a variety of colored buttons or all the same.

To Save You Time

http://tlc.howstuffworks.com/home/knitting-instructions10.htm

Homemade Beauty

What You Will Need

- For each girl, a list of recipes for homemade beauty products (such as lotions, shampoo, lip gloss, and bath salts)
- Ingredients to make a beauty product

What to Do

With the girls, make a beauty product. Make enough so that each girl can take some home and try it.

Basic Lip Gloss

½ ounce beeswax beads
4 ounces sweet almond oil
1 teaspoon colored jojoba beads
2 teaspoons essential oil

Put almond oil in glass measuring cup, then add beeswax beads and jojoba beads. Melt mixture in microwave. Stir with spoon. Let cool for a few minutes and then add essential oil. Pour into lip-balm jars and allow to set.

Cocoa-Butter Hand Lotion

2 cups warm water
1½ cup glycerin
½ ounce spirits of ammonia
½ ounce cocoa butter
½ teaspoon boric acid
1 cup stearic acid

Combine cocoa butter, glycerin, and stearic acid in a glass bowl. Melt over low heat in a pot of hot water. Carefully remove the bowl, then add ammonia. Stir until it becomes milky. Add boric acid to warm water. Add to first mixture. Mix with electric mixer for 10 minutes at high speed. Add perfume and color if desired. Allow lotion to age for two weeks before using.

Bath Salts

1 cup rock salt
1 tablespoon Epsom salt
¼ teaspoon mineral oil
1 to 2 drops food coloring
2 or 3 drops flavoring extract (watermelon, strawberry, vanilla, lemon, etc.)

Mix all ingredients together.

Body Glitter

3 tablespoons of unmedicated aloe vera gel
½ teaspoon very fine glitter
1 drop essential oil (optional)
Soap/lotion coloring (optional; do not use food coloring)

Add desired amount of glitter to aloe vera gel. If you are using coloring, mix a few drops at a time with gel until you get the desired color. Add essential oil if desired. Stir to blend thoroughly.

Store at room temperature in a small, airtight jar or container. Test the body glitter on the inside of your arm before applying to your face. *Do not use near your eyes.* NOTE: Some people are sensitive to essential oils.

Magnetic Checkerboards

What You Will Need

- Sheet metal
- Paint
- Glass accent marbles with one flat side (look in the floral section of a craft store)
- Hole punch (same size as the glass rock)
- Silicone sealer (found in the glue section)
- Scrapbook paper
- Round magnets
- Checkerboard stencil

What to Do

Magnetic boards: Make sure the sheet metal does not have any sharp edges. Paint a checker board pattern onto the sheet metal. (Use a stencil or make a stencil with cardstock or poster board). Checkers: Using the hole punch, punch out paper to use as checker (you will want all one color or pattern for "red" checkers and another pattern or color for "black" checkers). Next, using silicone sealer (a drop the size of a pencil eraser or smaller), glue the image to the magnet. Put a small drop of sealer in the middle of the picture. Lower the marble onto the picture and press down gently. Let it dry for about an hour before you put it on the checkerboard.

Variation

Make a decorative pushpin. Using the hole punch, punch out paper to use as your image on the push pin. Next, using silicone sealer (a drop the size of a pencil eraser or smaller) put a small drop of sealer in the middle of the picture. Lower the accent marble onto the picture and press down gently. Let it dry for about an hour before you put it on the pushpin. Glue a flathead pushpin behind the image and let it dry.

Engineering Lesson

What You Will Need

- Straws
- Play dough (buy it or make your own)
- Cup
- Pennies

What to Do

Have a lesson about what engineering is, or have an engineer come speak to the girls. Give each of the girls a handful of straws, a ball of play dough, and a cup. Using the materials you gave them, have them build a structure that will hold the cup off the table, right side up. Have girls work in teams or individually. (Encourage girls not to look at someone else's structure but to come up with their own ideas.) When their structures are ready, have the girls drop pennies into their cups one a time. Keep dropping pennies until the structure falls. See whose structure can hold the most pennies.

Public Speaking

What You Will Need

- Paper or cloth bag
- Random objects (for example, a shoe, a toy, a book, a bottle of shampoo, a tube of lipstick, etc.)

What to Do

Fill bag with the random objects you brought. Have each girl take one object. Give girls a few minutes to prepare. Then have each girl present a two-minute speech or commercial about the item she chose.

Variation

After each girl has given her two-minute speech, have all the girls use the random objects to put on a skit or do a commercial together. If you have a lot of girls, divide them into groups.

Learn about Native American Culture and History

What You Will Need

- Information about Native American culture and history
- Terra-cotta-colored clay (found at most craft stores)
- Colored beads

What to Do

Teach girls about Native American culture and history. Show girls pictures of pottery made by Native Americans. Give girls some clay to make their own pots. Put colored beads on the pots while they are still soft.

To Save You Time

http://nativeamericancultures.com/

Gardening Skills

What You Will Need

- Disposable cup or terra-cotta pot for each girl
- Soil
- Seeds to plant (herbs are fun)
- Items to decorate planting pot—markers, embellishments etc.

What to Do

Talk about what a seed needs to survive, how to transplant a seedling, and how to care for flowers and vegetable plants. Give each girl some soil, seeds, and a cup or terra-cotta pot. Have girls plant the seeds. If time, have girls decorate container.

Library and Literacy

What to Do

Ahead of time, call a nearby library and arrange for a librarian to take your group on a tour of the library. Have the librarian show your girls how to look up books on the computer. Have him or her explain how books can be categorized in types called genres, and talk about the different genres, such as mystery, suspense, romance, biography, science fiction, fantasy, fairy tales, folk tales, myths, historical fiction, realistic fiction, nonfiction, reference, poetry, etc.

Variation

Have the girls bring their library cards and check out some books. If any girls do not have a library card, help them get one (get parents' permission first).

Career Night

What You Will Need

- Guest speakers
- Props (optional)

What to Do

Have parents (or anyone who has an interesting job) come talk to the girls about their jobs (send around a sign-up sheet at priesthood and Relief Society). Have them tell the girls what responsibilities they have at their jobs, and what type of schooling and career they needed. Have the girls write down some of the careers they would like to pursue.

Variation

At an activity, have some of the ward members speak about the hobbies they enjoy. (If possible, send around a survey during Relief Society and priesthood.) Have the girls share their hobbies also.

Flag Etiquette

What You Will Need

- Your country's flag

What to Do

Teach the girls the proper way to fold a flag, the proper times to fly a flag, and the importance of respecting the flag.

To Save You Time

Flag information can be found in Boy Scout handbooks.

Learn the Basics

What You Will Need

- Iron
- Items to iron to show basic laundry skills
- Cleaning supplies
- Piece of scrap cloth and a button for each girl (or have the girls bring an item of clothing that needs to be mended)
- Thread and needle for each girl

What to Do

Teach the girls how to sort clothes (by color and by washing instructions), and how to do laundry. Show them how to iron various clothing items—shirts, dress, pants, etc. Show girls how to properly fold or hang a shirt, pants, etc. Have the girls practice their newly learned skills.

Teach the girls how to vacuum, mop, sweep, dust furniture, etc. Make it fun by having contests. (Could scatter crumbs on the carpet and have a vacuuming contest.) Share the prophets' teachings about how we should be industrious and clean. Explain how we can serve our family by helping with the housework.

Teach the girls some basic sewing skills—how to thread a needle, sew on a button, mend some clothing, etc.

Have an expert in organization come and talk to the girls about organizing their clothes closets and/or rooms.

Learn Dance Skills

What You Will Need

- Dance instructions (or find someone who knows how to dance to teach the girls)
- Music for the dances that will be taught

What to Do

Have the girls learn different styles of dance. Have an instructor come and teach a couple of kinds of dance, such as country swing, salsa, waltz, etc.

Guitar Lessons

What You Will Need

- A guitar for each girl (borrow as many guitars as you can)

What to Do

Have a guitar teacher give the girls a basic guitar lesson. If you don't have enough guitars for all the girls, have one group do the guitar lesson while the other girls do another activity you have planned. Then have the groups switch so everyone has a chance to do both activities.

Preparing for Young Women

Here are some extra activities for Preparing for Young Women. The girls are required to do all five goals in the *Faith in God* book, so these will not replace those goals (unless otherwise noted). Ideas may also pass off a goal in another area.

Breakfast or Lunch with the Young Women

What You Will Need

- Food for a breakfast or luncheon

What to Do

If possible, assign each Activity Days girl to a girl in your ward's Young Women organization. At an activity, seat girls and young women one-on-one at small tables. In advance, give your girls lists of questions they can ask the older girls, like "What is it like at Young Women's?" "What are some activities you do in Young Women?" "What is the Personal Progress Program?" etc.

Variation

Have each Activity Days girl fill out a questionnaire by asking her young woman the questions on the questionnaire. If you have time, have them switch places and have the girl from Young Women ask the same questions of the Activity Days girl. The questions should be questions that will help everyone to get to know one another better. After the girls have filled out the questionnaires, read them out loud and have everyone guess whom you are talking about.

You Are Special

What You Will Need

- The book *You Are Special*, by Max Lucado

What to Do

Read the book to the girls. Tell the girls how each of us is unique and that is what makes us special. When the girls are hard on themselves, it makes Heavenly Father sad, because He made every one of us, and He knows how special we each are (quote some scriptures to support what you are teaching). Talk about how we all have our own special talents. Talents are anything that we are good at, such as writing poems, playing the piano, always having a smile on our face, or being kind to others. Have each girl write down five talents she has. Make sure they don't just list the obvious ones like dancing, playing a musical instrument, etc. Tell girls NOT to put their names on the lists. Have girls put the lists in a basket and then randomly draw them out and read them.

Talk Ideas File

What You Will Need

- Various quotes and talks from prophets
- 3-ring binder
- Sheet protectors
- File dividers

What to Do

Most Young Women will have an opportunity to speak in sacrament meeting. Have girls prepare now by gathering information they can use in their talks. Have them collect quotes from prophets, and take notes on talks they hear in general conference, firesides, stake conference, or sacrament meeting. Have the girls organize the information by theme (such as faith, repentance, tithing, etc.). Have girls keep any handouts they receive in Primary or at Activity Days. Encourage girls to continue to add to their collection throughout their lives.

Learn How to Conduct Music

What You Will Need

- Learn how to conduct music, or ask someone who knows how to teach the girls

What to Do

If possible, make a handout showing the different time signatures for music: 4/4, 3/4, 2/2, 6/8, etc.

Tell the girls that as they enter into the Young Women program, they may be asked to conduct the music, so it's a great idea to learn now. Teach the girls or have your ward music specialist teach the girls how to lead music with several different time signatures. If you have time, teach girls how to read basic music notes. Have each girl practice leading the music.

To Save You Time

http://lds.org/cm/display/0,17631,4773-1,00.html

Article of Faith 13*

What You Will Need

- Small bean bag or ball
- Chalkboard or another way to write a list of things
- Large poster or individual copies of Article of Faith 13
- CD of inspirational music

What to Do

Start the activity by singing the Primary song "The Thirteenth Article of Faith." Have the girls recite the Article of Faith a few times. Talk to them about what the word "virtue" means. Have the girls sit in a circle and play the inspirational CD you brought. Begin having the girls pass around the bean bag or ball you brought. Then randomly stop the music. Whoever is holding the bean bag when the music stops must name something that is uplifting and virtuous. On the chalkboard or a piece of paper, write a list of the things named. Discuss them afterward. End with singing "The Thirteenth Article of Faith" again.

*This will pass off goal 1 under "Preparing for Young Women" ("after reading the thirteenth Article of Faith, make a list of things that are virtuous and uplifting").

Importance of Education*

What to Do

In advance, set up a tour of a local college. Ask the tour leader ahead of time if she will talk to the girls about the importance of college, which jobs require a college education, the importance of doing well in school now, how to obtain scholarships, and anything else you want your girls to know.

After, talk about ways a good education can help strengthen your home, family, and spirituality.

*This will pass off goal number 4 under "Preparing for Young Women—importance of a good education."

Alphabet Night

What You Will Need

- Prizes
- Food
- Invitations

What to Do

Pick a letter of the alphabet to be the theme of your party. Have all the girls bring a creative, unique item that starts with that letter. Have food and games or activities that start with that letter. Wear an item of clothing that starts with that letter. See examples below.

To Save You Time

Ideas for Letter-Themed Parties

H: Wear a hat, eat hot dogs, and play hang man or hide and go seek.
S: Wear crazy shoes, eat spaghetti, and sing songs.
V: Make a vegetable creature and eat vegetables.
P: Wear pajamas and eat pizza or pancakes.
W: Wear wacky clothes and eat watermelons (variation: make mini watermelons; recipe follows)

Recipe for Mini Watermelons

2 limes
1 small package red JELL-O®
Mini chocolate chips

Cut both limes in half lengthwise. Scoop out fruit with a spoon. Place the lime peels in a muffin tin to keep them from tipping over. Make the box of JELL-O according to the Jiggler directions. Spoon JELL-O into the limes halves. Chill until almost firm. Using a skewer, push the mini chocolate chips into the JELL-O to look like watermelon seeds. Chill until firm, then cut into slices.

Fruit Candy Game

What You Will Need

- Chewy fruit candy, like Skittles®

What to Do

Pour the candy into a bowl. Have the girls sit in a circle and pass around the bowl of candy. Have the girls take turns closing their eyes and picking two candies out of the bowl. If a girl picks two candies of the same color, she can chew and swallow them. If not, she must hold them in her mouth until she picks two candies that are the same color. Keep going around until the bowl is empty.

Creative Candy Bowling

What You Will Need

- Candy-coated chocolate pieces (like M&Ms®) or chewy fruit candy (like Skittles®)

What to Do

Take the girls bowling. Assign a different way to bowl for each candy color, such as red—granny style, yellow—backwards, blue—eyes closed, green—use opposite hand. Each girl picks a piece of candy without looking, then bowls using the technique assigned to that color of candy.

Variation

Fill two-litter pop bottles with water or sand. Make sure they are sealed tight so they don't leak. Use a ball and the two-liter bottles to bowl.

Party Quirks

What to Do

Take one girl ("host") out of room so she can't hear. Three volunteers ("actors") ask the rest of the girls what they should act out so that the host can guess what it is. (It could be something like "turning into Curious George," "a hitchhiker needing a ride to church," or "someone who really needs chocolate." For a gospel/scripture connection, it could be something like "a shepherd tending sheep," "a missionary preaching the gospel," "someone who has lost a piece of money or a pearl of great price.") The host comes back in the room, and the actors act out the characteristic or action, intermingling with each other. The host guesses what the three actors are trying to display.

Who Is "IT"?

What You Will Need

- Blank strips of paper for all your girls, with an X on one of them

What to Do

Put the strips in a bowl and have each girl pick a strip of paper without looking in the bowl. Once each girl has chosen a strip, have them look at the strips. Whoever has the one with the X is "it," but she doesn't tell anyone. Girls sit in a circle and hold hands. The girl who is "it" silently chooses a number, then squeezes the next girl's hand that many times. (If seven were the chosen number, the girl who is "it" would give seven squeezes to the next girl's hand.) That girl then squeezes the next girl's hand six times, who squeezes the next girl's hand five times, who squeezes the next girl's hand four times, and so on. The girl who only receives one squeeze is out. When a girl thinks she knows who is "it," she can accuse the girl, who must show her strip of paper to reveal whether or not she is "it." If she is wrong, she is out and the game continues. When the game ends, sit down and talk about it. Explain how there can be hidden dangers in life so we should obey the commandments and listen to our prophets and our parents when they warn us.

Getting-to-Know-You "Jenga" Game

What You Will Need

- Jenga (game)

What to Do

Ahead of time, type questions for about half of the Jenga pieces. Mod Podge®, tape or glue them onto the Jenga game pieces. At the activity play the game Jenga. When a girl pulls out a block with a question on it, everyone must stop and answer the question about herself.

Getting-to-Know-You Game

What You Will Need

- Chocolate
- Chewy fruit candy (like Skittles®) or any colorful candy (such as Starburst®, gummy bears, or jelly beans)
- Get-to-know-you questions (assign each question to a particular color of candy)

What to Do
Pass around a bowl of candy. Have each girl pick a piece of candy without looking, then answer a question according to the color of the candy.

To Save You Time
Red: What is your favorite scripture story?
Orange: What is your favorite food?
Yellow: What makes you happy?
Green: What country you would like to visit?
Blue: What goal you would like to achieve?
Brown: What item do you feel you couldn't live without?

Who Has . . .?

What You Will Need
- "Who has . . .?" paper (prepared ahead of time) for each person
- Pen or pencil for each person

What to Do
Play the "Who has . . .?" game. Ahead of time, prepare a list of items someone may have, may have done, etc. (For example, "Who has blue eyes?" "Who has traveled out of the country?") Give each person his or her own paper so everyone has to mingle to try to find someone who has done things on the list. When a guest finds a person with something on the list, he or she should have the person initial that thing or write his or her name by it. After a set amount of time, see who has checked off the most items on their list.

To Save You Time
Who has traveled out of the country?
Who knows how to sew?
Who has visited a farm?
Who has met a movie star?
Who has flown on an airplane?

Who has computer skills?
Who has been on TV (news, etc.)?

Princess Party

What You Will Need

- Movie *Princess Diaries*
- Cardstock to make a crown for each girl (or buy foam crowns at a craft store)
- Jewels, glue, etc., to decorate crowns
- Snacks

What to Do

Have a fun night watching the movie *Princess Diaries,* eating snacks, and letting the girls decorate their own crowns. Don't forget to take pictures.

Friendship Night

What You Will Need

- Games (have each girl bring her favorite)
- Snacks (have each girl bring her favorite)

What to Do

Have each girl bring her favorite game and snack. Spend the evening getting to know each other, playing games, and eating snacks.

Variations

- The week before, give each girl a large, blank piece of poster paper. Have her decorate it with pictures of herself and her family, and with things she likes. The next week when you meet, hang the posters around the room for everyone to look at, or each girl can hold up her poster and tell all about it.
- Put the girls' name in a basket. Pick two names out of the basket, or just pair the girls up. Give each girl a list of questions to ask her partner.

After each girl interviews her partner, have the girls tell what they have learned. This is a great chance for the girls to get to know each other.

Activity-Day Pen Pals

What You Will Need

- Nice paper for letter writing
- Pens

What to Do

Ask another group of Activity Days girls (in another ward, stake, or branch) to be pen pals with your girls. Have each girl write letters to her pen pal. After a few letters have been exchanged, invite the other girls to a joint activity with your girls.

Visit a Cemetery

What You Will Need

- Paper
- Crayons
- Questions, prepared ahead of time (optional)

What to Do

Go to the cemetery ahead of time and write down things for the girls to look for. (For example, "Find the grave with the bear on it," "Find the grave for a Bob R. Jones," "When did Carrie J. Larsen die?") Then take the girls to the cemetery and have them make crayon or pencil rubbings of inscriptions on the headstones or grave markers. Make sure the girls are supervised and show respect for the graves.

Play-Dough Pictionary

What You Will Need

- Play dough
- Words ahead time for girls to make out of play dough (for example, “cat,” “house,” “book,” etc.)

What to Do

Play Pictionary using play dough. Instead of having the girls draw their clues, have them use play dough to sculpt their clues.

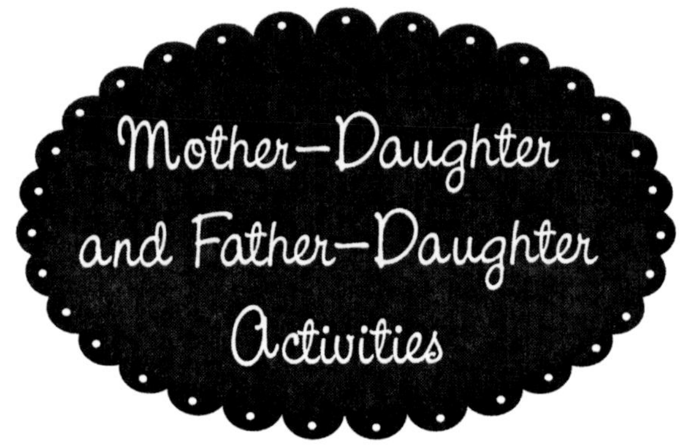

Many of these activities can be used interchangeably as a mother–daughter or father–daughter activity. Be sensitive of the girls who may not have a mother or father who can attend.

Concert or Museum

What You Will Need

- Find a local museum or a free concert the girls would like

What to Do

Plan a night where the girls, as a group, can go out "on the town" with their mothers or fathers. Have them dress in their Sunday best and attend a free concert or visit a local museum.

Fiesta Fun

What You Will Need

- Mexican food (such as chips and salsa for each table, ingredients to make tacos or taco salad)
- Latin music
- Materials to make party invitations
- Sombreros for pictures
- Decorations (brightly colored streamers and tablecloths)

- Terra-cotta pots lined with plastic wrap (use as serving dishes) (At an earlier activity, have the girls decorate the pots with a fiesta theme, using foam paint, markers, colored beads, jewels, etc.)
- Materials for games (choose from list under "What to Do")

What to Do

Have a fiesta party with the girls. A couple of weeks in advance, make fun invitations and send to the girls and whichever parent will be invited. At the party, eat Mexican food, take a picture of each girl with her mom or dad (each wearing a sombrero, of course), and do some of the following activities.

Rojo, Verde: Spanish version of red light, green light. The game is played just the same, except that "it" says "verde" instead of "green light," to tell players to go. To stop the other players, she says "rojo" instead of "red light."

Musical Chairs: Use fun, festive Latin music.

Hot Pepper Game: Just like the game Hot Potato, only using a pepper (don't use a spicy pepper as it may break open and burn the girls' fingers).

Pin the Tail on the Donkey: Get a poster or large cutout of a donkey, then blindfold girls and have them pin a paper tail on the donkey, using pushpins.

Macarena: In advance, teach the girls this fun line dance. At the party, they can help teach the dance steps to their fathers or mothers.

Variations

- Make a sombrero cake. Use a 10-inch round cake as the base of the sombrero. Use a two-cup glass measuring cup to bake the cake that will be the peak of a sombrero. Decorate "hat" with light chocolate frosting. Make a zig-zag pattern on the hat using frosting or red string licorice.
- At the fiesta or another activity, make frames to hold the pictures you took at the party. Buy cheap wooden frames and small glass tiles, in fiesta colors if possible—red, green, etc. Use the tiles and frames to make mosaic frames.

- Make piñatas. Provide the girls and their mothers or fathers with several empty boxes of various sizes, empty toilet paper and paper towel rolls, and various colors of crepe paper, plus glue and scissors. Have them work together to make piñatas. Can fill with candy and play the piñata game. Make sure you take pictures.

Cruise around the World

What You Will Need

- Decorations from countries you will focus on

What to Do

In advance, assign each girl to bring a food from another country and be prepared to tell a few things about that country. Ask ward members or girls if they have any decorations they can bring. At an earlier activity, have each girl make the flag of country she was assigned. Have the girls learn the song "Children All over the World" (see "music" on lds.org). Have girls sing the song the night of the activity. For the actual event, have the girls and their mothers or fathers dress in costumes from another country. Have each table decorated with items from a different country. Hang the flags the girls made, or use the flags for table decorations. Have a buffet of the different foreign foods the girls brought. Have each girl take a few minutes to explain what she learned about the country she was assigned, or have girls prepare posters ahead of time or at a previous activity. Hang the posters around the room. Serve nachos for Mexico, orange chicken or mini egg rolls and fortune cookies for China, fresh fruit and teriyaki chicken for Hawaii, croissants or bread and cheese for France, pizza or spaghetti for Italy.

To Save You Time

First Stop: Mexico (have a piñata, dance to Mexican music)
Second Stop: China (make Chinese fans, write names in Chinese characters, see how many gummy worms or gummy fish the girls and fathers or mothers can pick up with chopsticks)

Third Stop: Hawaii (give everyone a Hawaiian lei and teach guests how to do a simple hula dance)
Fourth Stop: France (provide paper and colored pencils or markers and have them create their own "Monet")
Fifth Stop: Italy (make Venetian masks [buy a paper or foam mask for each girl, and provide jewels and feathers to decorate the masks])

Mother–Daughter Super Saturday

What You Will Need

- A variety of simple crafts

What to Do

Have an activity similar to a Relief Society Super Saturday. Have a variety of crafts the girls can choose from. In addition to free, simple crafts, you might want to include a few more complicated crafts (girls would sign up ahead of time for these, and they would have to pay for the supplies). Could combine with the Young Women and their mothers for this activity.

To Save You Time

www.tipjunkie.com/super-saturday-craft-day/
http://supersaturdayldscrafts.blogspot.com/

Mother-and-Me Breakfast

What You Will Need

- Ingredients to make a simple breakfast

What to Do

Have the girls invite their mothers to a breakfast. If possible have the girls make and send out invitations ahead of time. Have everyone (including leaders) wear pajamas. Have a list of questions to ask mothers and daughters about themselves (you will need to call them ahead of time and privately ask them these questions).

Variation

Have each mother and daughter bring a baby picture of herself. Have everyone match mothers' baby pictures with daughters' baby pictures.

Mother–Daughter Progressive Dinner

What You Will Need

- Ingredients for a simple four-course meal, such as salad, breadsticks, spaghetti, and dessert
- Four people willing to provide a dinner course at their house
- Menu that tells where each course will be served
- Spiritual message or thought to read at each house

What to Do

Have everyone meet at the first-course house. Hand out menus, then eat and have a spiritual thought. Proceed to the rest of the houses, eating and having a spiritual thought at each one.

Mother–Daughter Hot Chocolate Party

What You Will Need

- A variety of hot chocolate mixes (mint, orange, raspberry, etc.)
- Mini marshmallows
- Cute hot chocolate mugs
- A variety of cookies
- Materials to make invitations

What to Do

At an earlier activity, have the girls help plan the party and make the invitations. Talk about manners and have the girls practice them at the party. At the hot chocolate party, have the girls and their mothers dress in their Sunday best and use their best manners. Serve hot chocolate and cookies, and have everyone mingle as they eat.

Variations

- Make homemade marshmallows (see www.marthastewart.com/recipe/best-homemade-marshmallows).
- Have a summer theme party. Serve lemonade and cookies.

Mother–Daughter Fashion Show

What You Will Need

- Large black and white garbage bags
- Materials to make a "fashionable" dress (bed sheets, fabric, ribbon, scissors, tape, straws, paper, string, crepe paper, etc.)

What to Do

Using the materials provided, have each girl design and make a dress for her mother to wear. Have each girl write a description of her mother's outfit. Have the mothers model their outfits in a fun fashion show. Assign someone to be the announcer and read off the description of the mothers' outfits as they walk down the "runway."

Mother–Daughter Book Club

What You Will Need

- A few months in advance, choose an appropriate book for mother and daughter to read
- Questions about the book (for discussion)

What to Do

At an activity, have the girls help pick a book they would like to read. After you read the book to make sure it is approriate, get copies at your local library for all your girls. Have them read the book at home with their mothers. Pick a date for your book club that gives everyone enough time to finish the book. Hold the book club at someone's house. Discuss the book and serve refreshments.

To Save You Time

Read, Remember, Recommend for Teens: A Reading Journal for Book Lovers, by Rachelle Rogers Knight (contains 2,500 award-winning and notable reading suggestions)

Mother–Daughter Fondue Party

What You Will Need

- Fondue pots
- Various dessert sauces for dipping (see recipes under "To Save You Time")
- Foods to dip (strawberries, pineapple chunks, orange slices, pretzels, marshmallows, brownies, cookies, graham crackers, cinnamon bears, etc.)

What to Do

At an earlier activity, have each girl write a letter to her mother. Collect the letters. Without the girls knowing, call each girl's mother and ask her to write a letter to her daughter. Collect the letters from the mothers. The night of the mother–daughter fondue party, set up the various fondue pots and dipping food. Just let the girls and mothers mingle and eat. When everyone is done eating, hand out the letters the mothers and daughters wrote to each other.

To Save You Time

Chocolate Fondue

1 cup heavy cream
12 ounces semi-sweet chocolate chips
1 teaspoon vanilla

Heat cream in a medium saucepan over medium-low heat until hot, about 2 to 3 minutes. When hot, add the chocolate and stir until it is just melted and smooth. Stir in vanilla. Move to a warm fondue pot.

White Chocolate Fondue

¾ cup heavy cream
12 ounces white chocolate chips
1 teaspoon vanilla

Heat the cream in a medium saucepan over medium-low heat until hot, about 2 to 3 minutes. When hot, add the chocolate and stir until it is just melted and smooth. Stir in vanilla. Move to a warm fondue pot.

Berry Fondue

1½ pounds fresh or frozen berries
¼ cup sugar

Place the berries in a food processor or blender and purée until smooth. Press the purée through a strainer or cheesecloth (to remove the seeds) and into a medium saucepan. Add the sugar and heat until the sugar has dissolved. Put into a warm fondue pot.

50's Night Father-Daughter Date

What You Will Need

- Materials to make invitations
- Decorations
- Food
- Music from the 1950's
- Bubble gum
- Hula hoops

What to Do

At an earlier activity, have the girls make the invitations and plan the 50's night. Have them plan the food and activities, and then make assignments of who will bring what. For the party, have the girls and their fathers dress in 50's attire. Decorate the room with old 45-rpm records, or have the girls make records out of black paper. For food, serve hamburgers or hot dogs, fries or chips in red-and-white-checkered paper containers, and root beer floats. Use old LP records as place mats (you can find these at second-hand stores like Deseret Industries). Activity ideas include dance contest, hula-hoop contest, bubble-blowing contest, hot-wheel drag race (race 50's-style play cars across floor, or blow across floor with straws). Have someone teach the girls and their fathers a few dances from the 50's.

Variation

Have everyone dress in 70's attire. Play 70's music, and if possible teach some 70's dances like "The Hustle," "Stayin' Alive," or "YMCA." Take pictures of the girls with their fathers. Make tie-dyed shirts at an earlier activity for the girls and their dads to wear.

Father–Daughter Hike

What You Will Need

- List of items for dads and daughters to find on the hike
- Water bottles (have each person bring his or her own)
- Trail mix or other snack

What to Do

Take a small nature hike on a local trail. Give each father–daughter team a list of several items they need to find while hiking.

Varation

Have the girls play a sport with their fathers (for example, basketball at the church building, or baseball, soccer, or football at the park). Provide drinks and snacks for everyone.

Who's Who? Father–Daughter Date

What You Will Need

- Several large blankets or rolling chalkboard
- Tools (hammer, screwdriver, wrench set, power drill, etc.), with a list of their prices (bring the tools from home or borrow them)
- Makeup, jewelry, and other "girly" items, with a list of their prices (bring the items from home or borrow them)
- Paper
- Crayons

What to Do

At an earlier activity, have each girl draw a picture of her father. At the father–daughter activity, hang the pictures around the room and have the fathers pick their pictures. Before the activity, string up some blankets or set up a few rolling chalkboards. Have the fathers go behind the blankets or chalkboards with only their bare feet showing. Have each girl guess which feet are her father's. Then switch places and have each father guess which feet belong to his daughter. Play a price-guessing game: lay out the tools you brought and have the girls guess the prices. Next it's the fathers' turn to guess the price of the various kinds of makeup, jewelry, and other girly stuff you brought. Serve a simple dinner like spaghetti. (Girls can help prepare dinner ahead of time.)

Variation

Have each girl bring her father's favorite dessert. Don't tell the fathers about the desserts. Have the mothers bring the desserts to a leader's house ahead of time so the dads don't see them. Have the girls go in the kitchen and serve their dads their favorite dessert. Then bring out the desserts and leave on a table so everyone can sample all the desserts.

Father–Daughter Western Barbecue

What You Will Need

- Food for barbecue
- For each person, a water bottle with a piece of bandana around the neck and a miniature cowboy hat on the lid
- Party favors (wrap in a bandana, then tie with twine)
- Disposable pie pans, to use as dinner plates
- Invitations (can use jean pockets with a bandana folded inside as your invitation "envelope")
- Getting-to-know-you activity prepared in advance (you will need large index cards, a marker or pen for each girl, and a list of questions to ask the fathers and daughters about each other)

What to Do

Meet at the park and grill hamburgers or hot dogs. Play the getting-to-know-you game. Start by giving each girl a few index cards and a pen. Ask the girls a question about their fathers (such as "What is your dad's favorite color?" or "What is your dad's favorite TV show?"). Have each girl write her answer on a card, without letting her dad see her answer. After the father answers the question, the girl holds up the card to show if she guessed right. Continue with several more questions. Then ask each father a question about his daughter and have him write down his answer. The girl answers the same question and the father holds up the card to see if he got it right. Do several questions.

Pizza Party Father–Daughter Night

What You Will Need

- Pizza crust, pre-made small pitas (without pockets), or frozen rolls
- Pizza sauce
- Cheese

- Toppings (have each girl bring her favorites)
- Rolling pins or 6-inch dowel rods (for rolling out pizzas)

What to Do

Have each father and daughter team work together to make their own pizzas. While pizzas are cooking, play "Pizza Roll" in father–daughter teams. Provide a pizza set for each team. Use paper or felt to make game pieces—the dough (a round circle in tan), sauce (smaller round circle in red), cheese (off-white or orange pieces), pepperoni (small red circles), mushroom (small brown circles), and green peppers (small green strips). Provide a die, or multiple dice if you want to speed the game up. Each team takes turns rolling the dice. A team must roll a 1 for the dough, 2 for the sauce, 3 for the cheese, 4 for the pepperoni, 5 for the mushroom, and 6 for the green peppers. If a person rolls a 1, that father–daughter team gets to put down the dough. Until a 1 is rolled, the team cannot get started making their pretend pizza. Teams must place the ingredients on their "pizza" in numerical order—first the dough (1), then the sauce (2), then the cheese (3), then the pepperoni (4), etc. A team only rolls the dice once, and then it is the next team's turn.. If a team doesn't roll the number they need, they must try again on their next turn.

Variations

- Have the girls decorate paper aprons.
- For dessert, make cookie pizza: In advance, make a mini cookie-dough crust for each person. Let them make their own dessert pizzas. Use melted chocolate for sauce. Top with candy-coated chocolate pieces (such as M&M's®), marshmallows, nuts, chewy fruit candies (such as Skittles®), or whatever you want to bring. Place fruit pizzas in oven for about seven minutes or until everything is melted, or just eat as is.

Go Fly a Kite

What You Will Need

- Materials to make kites
- Ingredients to make breakfast

What to Do

Have the girls help make and serve breakfast for their fathers. Then have each girl work with her father to make and decorate a simple kite. Go fly kites outside.

To Save You Time

www.ehow.com/how_4761472_make-simple-kite-kids.html
http://familyfun.go.com/crafts/20-minute-kite-670372/

Father–Daughter Halloween Party

What You Will Need

See below

What to Do

Food Ideas

Mummies: Skewer two large marshmallows on a pretzel stick, then wrap in a long piece of fruit leather. Roll in sugar so they don't stick together.

Chocolate monsters: Melt chocolate and butterscotch chips, then mix with chow mein noodles and drop on wax paper to cool. Use small orange or yellow chocolate candies for the eyes.

Mummy dogs: Wrap hot dogs in croissant dough or bread to look like a mummy, then bake.

Monster cupcakes: Place coconut (colored or toasted) in a bowl. Frost each cupcake, then dip frosted top in bowl of coconut. Place cupcake right side up on a tray and add a variety of candies to make monster features on the cupcake.

Activities

Squash bowling: Use butternut squash as the pins and a small pumpkin as the bowling ball. For party favors: fill crepe-paper pumpkin pouches with candy.

Make a pumpkin pouch: Cut two 10-inch-diameter circles from orange crepe paper. Stack circles and put candy in the center. Pull sides of paper up around candy to form a pouch. Gather paper just above the treats, then twist a little. Secure by wrapping green floral tape around the base of the twist, binding upward to create pumpkin stem. If necessary, trim extra paper before binding.

Father–Daughter Fear Factor

What You Will Need

- See activities under "What to Do" (Remember, they are meant to be disgusting!)

What to Do

Make sure everyone wears clothes they don't mind getting dirty. Do a few of the following activities:

What a Baby!: Bring mini jars of gross flavors of baby food (peas, squash, green beans, etc.). Have girls and daughters draw a jar from a basket and eat the baby food.

You're a Lifesaver: Blindfold a person and give him or her a lifesaver candy. Have the person suck on the candy and guess what flavor it is.

Blind Man: Blindfold the father or daughter. Have the seeing person guide the blindfolded one through a simple maze or obstacle course without touching the person. (Prepare maze or obstacle course ahead of time.)

Eew, Gross!: Do this activity in the gym. Fill a large bowl, bucket, or mini swimming pool with overcooked spaghetti noodles (can add tomato sauce and/or vegetable oil). Mix plastic bugs or gummy worms into the spaghetti. See how many bugs or worms the girls and fathers can find in one minute. You may need to put the bugs back in for the next person.

Variations

- Before the activity, put different-colored pieces of paper, fabric, or flags in a dark room. (Use a classroom and black out the windows with black paper.) Assign each a team a different color. As a group or as teams, have them go in the dark room for a certain amount of time, to see how many of their "flags" they can find in the time limit. You can provide each team a small flashlight.
- Serve a "cow pie": Make a pan of brownies. Cut them up and smash the pieces together to make a mound. Then pour hot fudge on top and place big plastic flies all over the mound.

July 24th

Pioneer Activity

What You Will Need

- Materials to make rag dolls, butter, or candles (for detailed instructions and lists of materials you will need, see internet links under "To Save You Time")

What to Do

If possible, have girls come to activity dressed as pioneers. Assign them a few weeks in advance to tell a pioneer story from their family or from someone in Church history. (Help girls that have a hard time finding one). Talk to the girls about how much the pioneers sacrificed to worship as they pleased, and how much our religion must have meant to them. Have the girls make crafts the pioneers may have made, such as corn-husk dolls or simple rag dolls. For a simple rag doll, you should cut and sew doll ahead of time, then have the girls stuff the dolls and add the face, hair, etc. For the dress, provide a scrap of fabric that the girls can wrap around the doll and tie with a ribbon, so that no sewing is involved.

To Save You Time

www.netw.com/~rafter4/nettie.htm (rag doll)
www.ci.tumwater.wa.us/researchcornhuskdoll.htm (corn husk doll)

www.ci.tumwater.wa.us/researchwhirligig.htm (whirligig, button toy)
www.ehow.com/how_5516614_make-pioneer-crafts.html (soap and candles)

Pioneer Games

What to Do

Play marbles, button on a string, or cat's cradle (yarn game). Or do activities like a stick pull, a three-legged race, a sack race, or a hog call (see who can do the best hot call). Here are the instructions for some other pioneer games and activities.

Wagon Pull: Find wagons or something the kids could pull—sleds, pieces of cardboard, laundry baskets etc. Form teams. One girl gets on the "wagon" and the other girl must pull her to the finish line.

Who Has the Button?: Have the girls form a circle. The person who is "it" leaves (or closes her eyes) while the others pass a button or another object around the circle. One person hides the object behind her back or in her lap. All the other players put their hands behind their backs (or on their laps) too. Then "it" is has three guesses to guess who is hiding the object. If "it" guesses correctly, she changes places with the girl who had the button, and that girl is "it."

Make a Log Cabin: Give the girls stick pretzels, some frosting, and a small clean, empty milk (or cream or buttermilk) carton. Have girls use the frosting as glue and the carton as the cabin base, gluing the pretzels to the cartons to make a log cabin.

Shadow Tag: One person is "it" and chases the others, trying to step on their shadows. (The pioneers loved to play this game on a sunny day.)

Pioneer Foods

What to Do

Have the girls make a food item the pioneers would have made, such as taffy, butter, or cornbread (johnny cake).

To Save You Time

http://www.pioneerthinking.com/vk_taffypull.html (taffy pull)

Johnnycake (a favorite dish of the Prophet Joseph Smith)

3 cups cornmeal
1 cup flour
2 teaspoons baking soda
1 teaspoon salt
2 tablespoons molasses
3 cups buttermilk
2 well-beaten eggs

Mix dry ingredients together. Slowly stir in molasses and buttermilk. Mix well. Add eggs and beat hard for two minutes. Pour into shallow, well-greased pans. Bake at 400°F for 30 minutes.

Buttermilk Doughnuts (President Brigham Young loved these)

2 cups buttermilk
1½ cups sugar
2 eggs
3 tablespoons butter
1½ teaspoons nutmeg
½ teaspoon baking soda
¼ teaspoon baking powder
½ teaspoon salt
flour

Combine ingredients, kneading in enough flour to make a soft dough that is not too sticky. Roll out and cut into doughnuts. Fry in deep, hot oil.

Homemade Butter

You will need some heavy cream and a jar with a lid. You can give everyone a clean baby food jar, or just use one large jar. Pass it around to the girls and have them each take turns shaking it until it turns to butter. To make it more like the butter the girls are used to, add salt and yellow food coloring.

Thanksgiving

Mini Cornucopias

What You Will Need

- Sugar ice cream cones
- Frosting
- Paper plate
- Piece of cardboard wrapped in foil
- Candy corn
- Pumpkin-shaped candy, or whatever candy you want

What to Do

Give each girl her own ice cream cone, a small amount of frosting, and some candy on a paper plate or foil-covered piece of cardboard. Spread frosting inside of cone, then fill with candy. Looks cute if candy spills out of cone.

Variation

Make a cone shape out of cardstock. Make or buy some pie crust or roll dough. Take dough and roll into ropes long enough to wrap around cone. Keep doing this all the way down until you have made a dough cone shape on the cardstock cone. (Can do individual ropes of dough or one large one.) Stuff cone with foil and bake, then remove paper and foil. Now you have a dough cornucopia. Let cool and then fill with candy.

Thanksgiving Place Cards

What You Will Need

- Cardstock (in Thanksgiving colors, if possible) cut into 4 x 4-inch or 5 x 5-inch pieces
- Markers
- Stickers and other embellishments

What to Do

Have the girls make place cards for everyone that will be at their Thanksgiving dinner. Have them fold the pieces of paper in half (so the place card will stand up on the table). Have girls write each person's name on a separate card, and decorate each card with markers or stickers. If they want, have girls put a small candy by each place card at the table, like candy corn or candy pumpkins.

Make Mini Pies

What You Will Need

- Mini foil pie tins
- Pie crust
- Pie filling

What to Do

Have each girl make her own mini pie. If you are really brave, help them make homemade pie crust.

Thanksgiving Pictionary

What You Will Need

- Chalkboard or whiteboard

What to Do

Play a game of Thanksgiving Pictionary. Have the girls take turns drawing something they are thankful for, while the others guess what they are drawing.

Thanksgiving Alphabet Game

What to Do

Have the girls sit in a circle. Have the first girl name something she is thankful for that starts with the letter *A*. Then, the next girl tells something she is thankful for that starts with the letter *B*. Keep going until you have done the whole alphabet.

Candy Acorns

What You Will Need

- Chocolate kisses (like Hershey's®)
- Light brown (or chocolate) frosting
- Mini vanilla wafer cookies
- Chocolate chips

What to Do

Using a dab of frosting, "glue" vanilla wafer to flat part of chocolate kiss. Put a dab of frosting on top, then add a chocolate chip for the stem.

CHRISTMAS

Create a Christmas Book

What You Will Need

- Coloring books
- Church magazines from December (older ones you are willing to let the girls cut up)
- Paper
- Pens and markers (or colored paper and stickers, depending on how you want to do pictures in book)

What to Do

Have girls create a book that tells the Christmas story. They can use the book to share the Christmas story with their family members and with younger children. Girls can draw the pictures, or you can provide pictures from coloring books, etc. Can use stickers and other embellishments. Have girls make the book cover out of cardstock or construction paper (could do a silhouette of Bethlehem on the cover). This activity lets girls be really creative. You could use photographs from the *Ensign, New Era, Friend,* etc. Instead of writing out the story in text, just tell who is in the photo or picture (for instance, the Wise Men), so the girls have to tell the story rather than read it. Make star-shaped sugar cookies.

Symbols of Christmas

What You Will Need

- Cookie dough
- Brief lesson about the symbols of Christmas
- Handout of the meaning of the symbols of Christmas (if possible, laminate the handout)

What to Do

Teach the girls about the symbols of Christmas (candy cane represents the staff of a shepherd, etc.). Each girl chooses her favorite symbol and creates a representation. Or you could choose one symbol, like the candy cane, and then you and the girls make candy-cane-shaped sugar cookies. (Can color or draw picture while cookies are baking.) Give the cookies to someone that is having a hard time and needs cheering up.

To Save You Time

Symbols of Christmas

Wreath: Eternal love—no beginning, no end
Candle: The light of Christ, our own inner light
Gifts: Giving, sharing, thinking of others
Bow: Bonds of goodwill to others
Bell: Rings to bring lost sheep home
Tree: The evergreen of everlasting life, pointing heavenward
Candy cane: Shepherd's crook for bringing lambs back to the fold
Star: The star of Bethlehem, a sign of prophecy, the light of the world

Variation

Have each girl make all the Christmas symbols out of play dough. Bake or let dry and then paint. Give each girl a handout that tells what each symbol means. Provide girls with a container to put everything in. Encourage them to tell the story at a family home evening.

Twelve (or Seven) Days of Christmas

What You Will Need

- Inexpensive Nativity set
- Copy of the Nativity story

What to Do

Pick a family in your ward. Assign each girl a day and give her one piece of the Nativity set. It is now her responsibility to secretly drop off her item to the family you picked, on the assigned day. Soon the family will have a full Nativity set. Give the family a copy of the Nativity story on the first or last day.

Variations

- Have the girls paint a ceramic Nativity set.
- Buy an inexpensive Nativity set for each of your Activity Day girls. Secretly drop off one piece of the set to each girl until she has the whole set. Make sure you also give each girl a copy of the Nativity story. On the last day, also drop off a treat and a Christmas card saying the Nativity set is from you.

Christmas Ornaments and Singing at Nursing Home*

What You Will Need

- Simple Christmas-tree ornaments (buy or make them)

What to Do

Buy or have the girls make some Christmas-tree ornaments (even simple glass balls). Have the girls go caroling at a local nursing home and pass out the ornaments to the residents.

*Also passes off goal in Serving Others.

Christmas Present Relay

What You Will Need

- A pair of gloves
- Wrapped box, tied with a ribbon

What to Do

Divide into two teams. The first girl of each team runs from the starting line, puts on an oversized pair of work gloves, and proceeds to untie a wrapped box. After doing this, she returns to her team and hands the gloves to the next team member. That team member puts on the gloves, runs to the box, and rewraps and reties it. This continues, with players wrapping the box until everyone has had a turn.

Variation

Have a relay to see who can wrap a present the fastest.

APRIL FOOL'S DAY

Activity Day "Test"

What You Will Need

- Copy of April Fool's test (below) for each girl
- Pen or pencil for each girl
- Blank sheet of paper for each girl

What to Do

Tell the girls that today is test day, and you hope they studied! Then give them the April Fool's test (below). After girls finish the test, talk about the origins of April Fool's Day and the traditional pranks played on that day. You can also talk about how April Fool's Day is celebrated in other countries.

April Fool's "Test"

DIRECTIONS: This is a timed test. You will be allowed only two minutes to complete it; therefore, you must work quickly. Record your responses on this sheet of paper.

1. Read everything before you do anything.
2. Print your name in the upper right corner of your paper.
3. Draw three triangles in the lower right corner.
4. Place an *X* in one square and an *O* in the other.
5. Write your age in the lower left corner.
6. Print today's date under your name.
7. Draw three circles in the upper left corner of your paper.
8. Divide each circle in half by drawing a line through the center horizontally.

9. Sign your name in the lower right corner.
10. Draw a square around your signature.
11. Write your birthday above your signature.
12. Now that you have finished reading everything, do only as directed in the first sentence. APRIL FOOLS!!

CHINESE NEW YEAR

Chinese Hair Sticks

What You Will Need

- Chopsticks (inspect them and sand any that have splinters)
- Paint
- Fine-tip paint brushes
- Paper plates (for paint)
- Cups (for rinse water)

What to Do

Have each girl use paint to decorate a pair of chopsticks. Tell girls to take their time and use a lot of details when painting. When they are finished, they now have Chinese hair sticks! Let the hair sticks dry, then take a picture of the girls wearing them. For refreshments, serve children-friendly sushi: Make Rice Krispies® marshmallow treats. While the mixture is hot, spread a thin layer onto a fruit rollup, put some gummy fish onto the marshmallow treat, then roll it all up into a "sushi" roll.

HALLOWEEN

Halloween Stories

What You Will Need

- Halloween story starters
- Paper
- Pens

What to Do

Give the girls a list of Halloween story starters. Have each girl choose one or as many as she wants and create a fun, scary, or silly Halloween story. If time, have girls illustrate their stories. Compile all the stories in a book for each girl.

Variations

- Sit in a circle. Start by saying a story starter. Then go around the circle and let everyone add to the story.
- Make a children's book version of the girls' stories. Have girls write a few sentences on each page, then illustrate each page. Have girls make a cute cover (laminate if possible), and bind the pages together into a cute Halloween book.
- Do any of the ideas above but change the theme to Christmas, Easter, Thanksgiving, or whatever you want.

To Save You Time

Some Halloween Story Starters

As I carefully entered the dark, haunted house, the door slammed behind me and . . .
It was a freezing cold Halloween night when . . .
The black cat started to hiss when . . .
The large cauldron of gross orange liquid started to boil and . . .
The mad scientist was creating a new creature that . . .
Something in the closet was making an eerie noise, so I opened the door and saw . . .
On Halloween, I was carving a pumpkin when . . .
The Halloween pumpkin slowly transformed into a . . .

Pumpkin Candy Character

What You Will Need

- Pumpkin for each girl

- Assortment of candy for decorating (mini marshmallows, thin black licorice [often called "laces" or "strings"], black jelly beans, etc.)
- Toothpicks

What to Do

Have each girl create a candy face on her pumpkin, using the toothpicks to attach the candy to the pumpkin. For example, mini marshmallows or black jelly beans would work great for a mouth, and licorice strings could be the hair or eyebrows.

Ghost Necklace

What You Will Need

- Parchment paper
- All-purpose school glue, such as Elmer's®
- Felt-tip pens
- String or ribbon

What to Do

Make a fun, simple, ghostly necklace. Give each girl a sheet of parchment paper and a container of school glue. Draw ghost outlines on parchment paper with the glue; let it set a few minutes. Fill the ghost in with more glue. Let the glue dry for two days, and then peel off. Draw face on ghost with a felt-tip pen. Punch small holes at the top, then weave string or ribbon through to make a cute necklace.

Pasta Skeletons

What You Will Need

- A variety of dried pasta
- All-purpose school glue
- Construction paper (black works best)

What to Do

Give each girl a sheet of construction paper, a variety of noodles, and some glue. Have girls create their own pasta skeleton. Girls can use alphabet-soup noodles to write names, etc., on their paper.

Pumpkin Seed Necklace

What You Will Need

- Large pumpkin
- Silk beading cord
- Threading needle

What to Do

Ahead of time, scoop out pumpkin and put the seeds and pulp in a bowl of water. (This will quickly separate the seeds from the fiber). Remove seeds, rinse them, and place them in a single layer on a paper towel or cookie sheet. Let the seeds dry at room temperature for six to eight hours. Do not let the seeds dry too long before stringing them or they will break easily and become hard to work with. On the day of the activity, give each girl some dried pumpkin seeds, and a needle threaded with silk beading cord. Have girls string the pumpkin seeds onto the beading cord, tying knots in between for spacing.

EASTER

Easter-Egg Memory Game

What You Will Need

- Matching pairs of colored eggs, dyed only on one side

What to Do

Set eggs face down in rows on the grass, white side up. The first player tries to find a match by turning over two eggs. If they match, she keeps them and goes again. If not, she turns them face down, and the next player is up. Girls keep taking turns until all the matches are found. Whoever finds the most matches wins the game.

Sticker Eggs Hunt

What You Will Need

- Plastic eggs
- Stickers (need two of each sticker)
- Candy to fill the eggs

What to Do

Put a sticker on each plastic egg. Spread the eggs out in the room you decide on, or outside. Leave them in plain sight. The girls will come in and think it is such an easy egg hunt. Then give them each a few of the stickers that match the one you put on the eggs. Now they must go find the eggs that match their sticker.

ST. PATRICK'S DAY

Lenny the Leprechaun Treasure Hunt

What You Will Need

- Leprechaun Footprints
- Treasure hunt clues
- Treasure for them to find

What to Do

Ahead of time, prepare treasure hunt clues (for example, "Go to where you would eat dinner"). Include recitations of the Articles of Faith. (For example, "Recite the fifth Article of Faith, then go where you would get a drink." The sink is where girls would find the next clue, and so forth.) When the girls come in, tell them that Lenny the leprechaun came to your house and left a treasure you need help finding. Then present girls with the first clue, and let the hunt begin. For the treasure, buy a black plastic cauldron (find at a party store), or use a black bowl, or a terra-cotta pot painted black. Fill with the treasure—chocolate gold coins or any gold candy. Could include (for each girl) a pencil, small notebook, nail polish, or anything you choose.

Variations

- Use individual black cauldrons instead of one large one.
- Make leprechauns' "magic powder." Pour a small box of pistachio pudding into a cellophane bag. Tie with a ribbon and have a tag on it that says, "leprechauns' magic powder." Then mix the pudding with milk according to package directions and watch as the white powder becomes green!

Leprechaun Hats

What You Will Need

- Sandwich cookies or vanilla wafers
- Marshmallows
- Melted white chocolate, colored green with food coloring

What to Do

Use one side of a sandwich cookie or a vanilla wafer, glue the marshmallow on top with frosting. Dip the whole thing in white chocolate that has been colored green. Use brown frosting to embellish.

WINTER

Winter Wonderland Party

What You Will Need

See "What to Do."

What to Do

Do one or more of the following.

Make paper snowflakes (will need paper and scissors).

Make snowmen. Use marshmallows and toothpicks, or Styrofoam balls and toothpicks or wooden skewers. Embellish with mini pom-poms (for eyes or nose), candy corn, black licorice, fabric for scarf, etc.

Play Pin the Nose on the Snowman.

Have an indoor snowball fight. Fill white socks with batting for snowballs.

Frost and decorate snowman or snowflake cookies. Serve with hot chocolate.

Snowman Game

What You Will Need

- Dice
- Red marker
- Chart that lists each snowman body part with a corresponding number
- For each girl:
    - 3 Styrofoam balls hooked together with a wooden skewer (to make snowman body)
    - Brads (for eyes), tops colored with permanent black markers
    - 2 toothpicks (for arms)
    - 3 thumbtacks for buttons (or use brads again, and color either black or multiple colors)
    - Piece of fabric for scarf
    - Piece of orange pipe cleaner for nose

What to Do

(This game is similar to the game Cootie, by Hasbro, where you build a plastic insect.) Post the chart on the wall. Each girl rolls the dice and, depending on the number she rolls, she adds the corresponding body part to her snowman. If she rolls the number of an item she has already added, she must wait until her next turn to try again. To make the game last longer, have a certain order in which girls must add items to their snowmen. For example: Must get eyes first, nose next, then mouth, and so on.

To Save You Time

Order for Adding Parts (to Make Game Last Longer)

Roll a 1: Snowman body
Roll a 2: Eyes (brads)
Roll a 3: One arm (toothpick)
Roll a 4: Other arm (toothpick)
Roll a 5: Buttons (3 thumbtacks or brads)
Roll a 6: Scarf (fabric)
Roll a 7: Nose (orange pipe cleaner)
Roll a 8: Mouth (use red marker to draw it on)

Mini Doughnut Snowmen Faces

What You Will Need

- Baby carrots (as small as possible)
- Black frosting or or black edible marker
- Mini doughnuts (such as Hostess)

What to Do

Insert a small baby carrot into the center of the doughnut for the nose. Using the frosting or marker, make dots to form two eyes and a mouth.

For Mother's Day: Make Paper Bead Necklaces

What You Will Need

- Scraps of colorful paper (gift wrap, magazine photos, or newspaper comics work best)
- Scissors
- Glue stick
- Drinking straws
- Yarn, ribbon, or string

What to Do

Have each girl make a necklace to give her mother for Mother's Day. To make each bead, cut a triangular strip of paper that measures about 1¼ inches across the base and 10½ inches from the base to the tip. Lay the strip face down on a piece of waxed paper or cardboard. Coat the surface of the paper with glue. Stick the base of the strip to the side of a drinking straw. Wrap the paper repeatedly around the straw, applying more glue, if necessary, to stick down the tip of the triangle. Once the glue dries, use scissors to cut away the straw on both sides of each bead. When beads are finished, string them on leather, yarn, nylon cording, ribbon, or string. Or use craft wire (available at craft and bead stores) to attach single beads to earring hangers.

Variation

Instead of having the girls give the necklaces to their mothers, have them donate the necklaces to a women's shelter. (Also passes off goal in Serving Others.)

Picture Frames

What You Will Need

- Photographs
- Inexpensive, basic picture frames
- Embellishments to decorate frames (jewels, foam shapes, stickers, etc.)

What to Do

Take photographs at a mother–daughter or father–daughter activity. Each girl will put her photograph in a frame, then decorate the frame and include a personalized note. Each girl can give the picture to her father for Father's Day, or her mother for Mother's Day, depending on who is in the picture with her.

Birthday Party

What You Will Need

- Birthday cake
- Party games
- Birthday card and small gift for each girl (for example: nail polish and file, small Primary songbook, journal, simple necklace)
- Party decorations
- Birthday card for each girl

What to Do

At the beginning or end of the year, have a big birthday party to celebrate all the girls' birthday. Have a birthday card for each girl and have the other girls sign it. Decorate the room with streamers and balloons. Have birthday cake, play party games, sing "Happy Birthday to You," and let the girls open the gifts you brought them.

Variation

- Have quarterly birthday parties. Celebrate all girls' birthdays from that quarter.
- Make or buy an individual cupcake for each girl. Put it in a decorative Chinese-food takeout container (available at craft stores).

Activity Day Binders

What You Will Need

- 3-ring binder (with a clear front pocket) for each girl
- Materials to decorate binder (fun paper, pens, markers, etc.)

What to Do

For each girl, print a personalized page for the clear front pocket of her binder. It could say, for example, "Emily's Activity Days Binder." Girls can use their binders to hold all their Activity Days handouts, etc. Put blank lined paper in the binders for girls to use as journal pages or to take notes. Have girls bring their binders every time you meet for Activity Days. Make sure you have a binder for each new girl as she comes into your group. Have an activity where girls put together and decorate their binders.

Variation

- For the first few minutes of each activity, have the girls write on their journal pages.
- In binders, include folders with pockets so girls can keep handouts without having to punch holes in them. (These folders are designed for three-ring binders and may be purchased at any office supply store.)

"Welcome to Activity Days" Cans

What You Will Need

- Large or small empty paint cans with lids (available at hardware stores or some craft stores)
- Items to fill cans (see below)
- Materials to decorate can (see below)

What to Do

Decorate the paint cans, using scrapbook paper, ribbons, stickers, jewels, etc. If possible put each girl's name on her can. Fill the can with a variety of "Welcome to Activity Days" items: scripture pencil, Articles of Faith bookmark or card, lip gloss, nail polish, candy, stickers, *Faith in God* booklet, birthday card, welcome letter from leader, list of leaders' phone numbers, scripture stickers, or whatever you want. This will be a welcome to Activity Days gift and a birthday gift all in one. Girls can use the can to hold anything special to them.

Caramel Corn for Dad

What You Will Need

- Ingredients for homemade caramel, or use the caramels you unwrap and melt
- Popcorn
- Cellophane bags
- Ribbon
- Stationery or blank greeting cards

What to Do

Have girls help you make caramel corn, then put the corn in cellophane bags and tie the bags with a cute ribbon. Each girl can write a letter or card to her father, then attach it to the bag of caramel popcorn and give it to him for Father's Day.

Personalized Hammers for Dad

What You Will Need

- Wood-handled hammer for each girl
- Sand paper
- Acrylic paints (any colors plus white)
- Paintbrushes
- Permanent, black fine-point marker
- Clear acrylic glaze or sealer

What to Do

Sand off any rough edges on the hammer. Paint one side of hammer white and let it dry. Then paint the other side white and let it dry. Girls can decorate the hammer with the colored paints, using the black marker to add details such as outlines or patterns. Let it dry for at least 30 minutes. In a well-ventilated area, have an adult spray the hammer with a clear sealant or glaze.

Charm Bracelet

What You Will Need

- Charms that correspond to the Activity Days goals
- Plain charm bracelet or necklace, or a large safety pin

What to Do

Hook the charms on a bracelet, necklace, or safety pin, or make a necklace out of ribbon. This is a great gift for birthdays, recognition nights, or for welcoming girls to Activity Days.

To Save You Time

www.charmingldsgifts.com/

Activity Days Scrapbook

What You Will Need

- Photos you have taken of the girls
- Simple scrapbook for each girl (such as a plain notebook, a binder filled with paper, or a small photo album)

What to Do

Take photographs of the girls at different Activity Day activities, and make multiple copies of the photos. Have each girl make a scrapbook.

Variation

Arrange the photos in a scrapbook or small photo album for each girl. This would make a great Christmas or birthday gift.

Scripture Pillowcase

What You Will Need

- White pillowcase for each girl
- White sheet (or something else you can cut up to make pockets)
- White thread

What to Do

Sew a pocket onto each pillowcase, big enough for a set of scriptures. Have girls put their scriptures into their pockets each day to remind them to read them every night.

The purpose of these events is to allow the girls to share what they have learned and accomplished. Invite both parents to Activity Days recognition nights.

Star-Theme Recognition Night

What You Will Need

- Invitations (shaped like a star or featuring a star)
- Star decorations
- Refreshments (star-shaped sugar cookies, star fruit, Starburst® candy, gold or yellow punch, etc.)

What to Do

Make sure everything about this night is star related, including the table decorations. Make the girls feel like the stars of the evening.

Paint Party Recognition Night

What to Do

For decorations, tape "splatters" of paint (paper cut in the shape of paint splatter) onto tablecloths. Place it on the sides of the tablecloths and on the floor to look like spilled paint. For centerpieces, use paint cans filled with paintbrushes, paint, etc. Use paper tablecloths so girls can use centerpiece paint and brushes to paint on tablecloths. For food, make "paint sample" cookie cards (make rectangle sugar cookies, then frost with four squares of various shades of one color). Or dip sandwich cookies into white chocolate that you have colored with various shades of food coloring. Or make a rainbow cake: Color white cake mixes with various colors and make single-layer cakes. Layer the cakes with white frosting in between each layer. When you cut the cake, you will see all the layers of color. Or swirl the different-colored cake mixes together in a pan and bake, so you will have swirled, multi-colored cake. For party favors, fill clear paint pans with colored candy (available at many craft stores).

Queen for a Night

What You Will Need

- A beauty-queen sash for each girl that says "Daughter of God" in glitter (make sashes yourself using 4- to 6-inch-wide craft ribbon, plus glued-on plastic jewels)
- A crown for each girl (make them or purchase toy crowns at a costume or party store)
- Dinner or refreshments
- Decorations
- Tablecloths

What to Do

At an earlier activity, have the girls make cute invitations (for their parents) using the queen theme. Ahead of time, ask each mother to write a few nice things about her Activity Days girl. (Make sure all girls have about the same number of things written about them, so no one feels bad.) Set up tables and decorate with nice centerpieces and tablecloths. Try to hold the activity in a gym where you have a stage. Have everyone dress in Sunday best. On the night of the activity, call the girls up on stage (or to the front of the room) one at a time. If possible, have a spotlight on each girl as you talk about her. Present her with her sash and crown, along with any awards she may have received. Read the nice things the girl's mother wrote about her, or just tell things about the girls to get to know them better (for example, Sarah's favorite color is red and she loves to write poetry, etc.).

Pajama Pizza Party

What You Will Need

- In advance, make a DVD with photos from previous activities (Have mothers give you a few candid shots of their girls, including baby pictures. Also include baby pictures of leaders.)
- Pizza
- Additional movie in case you have extra time

What to Do

Have everyone meet at a leader's house wearing pajamas. Eat pizza, watch the DVD you made, and, if time, watch a fun, clean movie. Hand out any awards girls may have earned, or have girls talk about or show goals they have accomplished.